Dam

D0332151

Titles in the *Objekt* series explore a range of types – buildings, products, artefacts – that have captured the imagination of modernist designers, makers and theorists. The objects selected for the series are by no means all modern inventions, but they have in common the fact that they acquired a particular significance in the last 100 years.

In the same series

Factory
Gillian Darley

Aircraft
David Pascoe

Motorcycle
Steven Alford & Suzanne Ferriss

Bridge
Peter Bishop

School
Catherine Burke & Ian Grosvenor

Dam

Trevor Turpin

REAKTION BOOKS

To Bill Turpin, an ingenious engineer (1920–2001)

Published by Reaktion Books Ltd
33 Great Sutton Street
London EC1V 0DX, UK

www.reaktionbooks.co.uk

First published 2008

Printed and bound in China

British Library Cataloguing in Publication Data
Turpin, Trevor
   Dam. - (Objekt)
   1. Dams - Design and construction   2. Dams - History
   I. Title
   627.8

   ISBN–13: 9 781 86189 328 4

Contents

	Introduction	7
1	Dam as Symbol and Function	16
2	Dam Designers and Builders	57
3	Dam Beauty and Dam Proud	106
4	Dam Failure	140
5	Dam Angry	170
6	What Environment?	203
	Postscript	233
	Glossary	236
	References	239
	Select Bibliography	249
	Acknowledgements	250
	Photographic Acknowledgements	251
	Index	252

Introduction

Water will overflow from the reservoirs in picturesque cascades . . .
forming probably the finest waterfall in this country.
James Mansergh[1]

These were the thoughts not of an artist but of one of the great British dam engineers of the nineteenth century. He was describing, in 1894, his perception of the Elan Valley scheme, which would provide water from the mountains of Wales to the flourishing English city of Birmingham, some 112 kilometres away. While his job was to create dams to store water for public supply and, ultimately, public health, it is clear that he saw in his designs the potential for structures that would add to and enhance the landscape.

John Muir, the founder in 1891 of the Sierra Club in the United States, and one of the early proponents of the idea of national parks, did not feel he needed dams to 'create' beauty – in fact he was committed to resisting them: 'Should Hetch Hetchy be submerged for a reservoir . . . it would be utterly destroyed [and] the sublime cañon way to the heart of the High Sierra would be hopelessly blocked.'[2] In the event, Yosemite *was* flooded to supply the city of San Francisco with water (perhaps surprisingly, while many dams have been built, more than 500 have been *removed* in the US, and today there are proposals to remove the dam that Muir fought against for many years). It is this tension between those who seek to respond to a community need and those who cannot countenance change that makes dams so fascinating.

Caban Coch in the Elan Valley – one of Mansergh's 'waterfalls', completed in 1904.

Dams come in all shapes and forms and serve a range of functions: water supply for public consumption, irrigation, generation of power, flood protection, navigation of rivers and provision of water to canals. Some contribute to the scene. Stand on the bank of the Thames at Woolwich in London, and the piers of the Thames Barrier, completed in 1982, rise from the murky river like a line of whales frozen in time. With their stainless-steel shrouds glistening in the rain, they have become, in less than 30 years, old friends to the populace of London whose lives, wealth and security they protect. However, climate change – a recurring theme in this book – means that the Barrier has a limited life span. Designed in the 1970s, it

Pen-y-Gareg dam, Powys, one of the nineteenth-century dams in the Elan Valley.

closed seven times in its first decade of operation but 38 in the second, and, as the polar ice caps melt, rising sea levels mean that new flood barriers will be needed for London by 2030. Love them or loathe them, dams will continue to play a vital role in our daily life.

If we travel just 16 kilometres upstream on the Thames towards Windsor Castle, we meet the reservoirs supplying drinking water to these same Londoners. No less useful than the Barrier, the reservoirs have been developed over the last hundred years or so. Their embankments are bland, boring and, in the sense of being unexplained, threatening. If the signs didn't say 'Keep Out', the railings and steep slopes surrounding them would. And yet behind these forbidding banks lie water bodies recognized internationally for the numbers and variety of wildfowl that call them home (or at least 'hotel'). Flanked by London's busiest motorway junction,

The piers of the Thames Barrier constructed between 1973 and 1982 to defend London from flooding.

Heathrow's terminals, sand and gravel pits and out-of-town super-stores, thousands of Gadwall and Shoveler arrive every autumn to feed and roost, oblivious to the human activity around them.

Dams are not new: the oldest, dating to 3000 BC, can be found north of Amman in Jordan. However, it was not until the Industrial Revolution that they were constructed in great numbers – first in Britain and eventually throughout the world. Initially they were built to provide a constant source of power for corn and cloth mills, belatedly – from the 1800s onwards – to meet the public-health needs of burgeoning cities. Today there are more than 45,000 large dams[3] throughout the world, but they are not evenly distributed, with most being in Europe, China, India and the US; China alone has more than 20,000.

Through a number of themes, this book addresses the range of emotions that dams generate. They can both inspire and dismay and the themes refer to these extremes. For example, the Hoover Dam was claimed by both Presidents Herbert Hoover and Franklin Roosevelt as a demonstration of a determination to 'do something'. J. B. Priestley recognized the dams on the Colorado River as representing a Brave New World. They satisfied and sustained the city of Los Angeles and spawned a new settlement, Boulder City, originally to house their 5,000 construction workers. Most of all, the Hoover Dam was a symbol of humanity's domination over nature: 'a mighty river, now a source of destruction, is to be curbed and put to work in the interests of society.'[4] But while engineers designed the structure of the dam, its ultimate appearance was determined by an architect, Gordon B. Kaufmann, with the sculptor Oskar Hansen. Not only the New Deal but the age of Modernism was also represented by the Hoover Dam. This alliance between the disciplines of art, architecture and engineering was to be enhanced in the latter half of the twentieth century by environmental specialists such as land-

scape architects and ecologists. We can also trace the development of industrial construction methods through the theme of dams – from navvies to automation. Finally, dams very occasionally appear in music, art and literature. David Constantine's *Under the Dam*[5] finds Shelley beneath Mansergh's 'Craig Ddu' reservoir, for example. Such associations are all the more surprising for being so rare.

Oskar Hansen's monument to the achievement of the Hoover Dam: two bronze figures (10 metres high) 'with the look of eagles', representing the settlers of the American West.

So we have emerging themes of symbol, literature, art, team-work and saviour. Then there is dismay. As one set of enthusiasts seeks to dominate nature, so another, dedicated to protecting and conserving it, is generated. While the dams that turned the California deserts green were welcomed by environmentalists in the 1930s, they did not require resettlement of the population. However, the same rivers that have traditionally given life to communities can easily take it away. The Three Gorges Dam on the Yangtze in China (first proposed in 1919) will require new homes for 1.4 million people; finding new agricultural land for the displaced farmers is an additional headache. Without these new dams, however, the flooding that claimed the lives of 300,000 people in the twentieth century alone would continue.

Communities have been prepared to die in attempts to halt the progress of dams. The Adivasi tribal peoples of Maharastra are India's oldest indigenous inhabitants. When the Sardar Sarovar Dam is finally completed on the River Narmada, many of them will be 'resettled'. However, the World Bank, which originally sponsored this hydropower and irrigation project, has now pulled out due to its dissatisfaction with the resettlement proposals. The culture of these people will disappear together with their gods and goddesses. As Booker Prize winner Arundhati Roy put it, 'This was the big one.'[6] Roy estimated that the people displaced by dams in India over the last 50 years could number 33 million. The World Commission on Dams (WCD), set up in 1998 to address such issues, put the worldwide number at between 40 and 80 million. Many have not been resettled or compensated.[7]

Once built, dams can *cause* death if not cared for and operated properly. One of the highest dams in the world, the Vaiont in Italy, built in 1961, today stands isolated as it curves across its valley – the water it once held flooded the villages downstream in 1983

following a landslide and cost hundreds of villagers their lives. The floodwalls and levees of New Orleans were neither designed nor maintained to withstand the Category-Four storm that Hurricane Katrina brought with it in August 2005. The consequent loss of life and devastation raised questions not only about engineering, but about the very nature of American 'civilization'.

Most of all, dams represent power: the generation of power, power over others, the power to create and maintain civilizations. As Lenin said in 1920, 'Communism is Soviet power plus the electrification of the whole country.'[8] Maintenance of civilizations is encapsulated by the story of the Nile, a river system draining several countries and supporting an ancient 'hydraulic' civilization. After leaving Ethiopia, the Blue and White Niles meet − the longest kiss in history − and flow through the Sudan to Egypt. Churchill, speaking in the 1890s, anticipated that the day would come when 'the Nile itself, flowing for 3000 miles through smiling countries, shall perish gloriously and never reach the sea.'[9] While the Aswan Dam was built (by the British, thus confirming their

The Three Gorges Dam on the Yangtze under construction in 2006.

interest and influence in Egypt), the Temple of Isis, which Churchill dismissed as somewhere for tourists to scratch their names, was saved, initially at least, by the ingenious engineers. The Aswan Dam was raised in height in 1912 and again in 1933; it was effectively replaced by the Aswan High Dam, completed in 1970. The resulting Lake Nasser covers 5,100 square kilometres and required the relocation of 150,000 people. This time, construction was financed by the Soviet Union just four years after the Suez Crisis, so the project is a striking symbol of Middle Eastern politics and the balance of world power at the time.

It may be that dams are now at a turning point: in the US they are being removed at an unprecedented rate (56 were decommissioned in 2005), while in developing countries they are still being created as quickly as ever (in 2006, in the Indian state of Himachal Pradesh alone, more than 40 dams (for hydropower) were proposed). How they are built places them centre stage in debates about

The Aswan High Dam on the Nile, completed in 1970, then the largest rock fill dam in the world (3,600 m long and 111 m high); 34,000 workers were employed in construction at its peak.

environmental issues – it is no longer acceptable to say, as the Indian Finance Minister Moraji Desai said in 1961, 'if you move, it will be good, otherwise we shall release the waters and drown you all.'[10] From early beginnings in the nineteenth century, worldwide environmental legislation, and a plethora of policies, programmes and conventions, ensures that today the effects of proposed dams can be assessed, and battle lines drawn, before construction starts. Dams can and have been stopped: in the 1950s, plans to dam and flood the Grand Canyon were halted by the conservation lobby – surely, with the benefit of hindsight and experience of other dams since on the Colorado, an action many would be grateful for! However, if planned carefully dams have a vital role to play in addressing climate change – they can provide renewable energy, protect river habitats, protect us from floods from increasing storm events, and store water for irrigation and supply in times of drought. After 5,000 years, their time has come.

Dam examines the key twenty-first-century issues of environmental legislation, sustainability and climate change through the themes of symbol, design teamwork, beauty, safety, anger and the environment. In this way, hopefully, the profile of a vital yet neglected feature of modern life will be enhanced.

1 Dam as Symbol and Function

Look on my works, ye Mighty, and despair!
Percy Bysshe Shelley

When Shelley penned this line, he could have had little idea of how prophetic it was to prove. In 1811 and 1812 he stayed in the Elan Valley in mid-Wales, first at Cwm Elan, where he described the scenery as 'a very great bore', and then at Nantgwillt, where he hoped to set up a commune. He wrote to his cousin, 'we are now embosomed in the solitude of mountains, woods and rivers, silent, solitary and old . . . '[1]

By 1904 James Mansergh had built the first three dams of the Elan Valley scheme for the water supply for Birmingham, and Cwm Elan and the Nantgwillt farmhouse were no more. These dams not only provided fine waterfalls but also were designed 'to harmonize with their situations . . . [and] . . . add to the beauty of the scenery'.[2] Mansergh also permitted himself a little Victorian adornment: the Foel Valve Tower is circular with a copper dome in the Birmingham Baroque style.

This chapter considers what dams symbolize as well as their intended functions: there is more to these confident masonry structures than just the granite. The Elan Valley dams were built on Welsh soil for the benefit of an English town, and to some they symbolized English dominance. The Welsh MPs Sir Hussey Vivian and Thomas Ellis contested that Welsh water should be left for

Welsh people, a view the *Birmingham Daily Post* saw as 'opposition seemingly on the dog in the manger principle namely that Welsh water which Wales does not want and cannot use ought not to be used . . . in England'.[3] However, it wasn't just Birmingham that coveted the Principality's resources – the scheme was also opposed by London, which wanted the water for itself! In the twentieth century, in the eyes of the Welsh Nationalists, Plaid Cymru, the presence of English water companies highlighted the political impotence of Wales within Britain.

In the event, four dams were built, the final one at Claerwen in 1952 replacing three others originally proposed by Mansergh's scheme. In 1973 a further plan to build a 95-metre-high dam above Caban Coch was put forward but not pursued.

The Birmingham scheme was not the first to have an imperial flavour to it. That honour went to the city of Liverpool, which completed Lake Vyrnwy in 1892. Designed by George Deacon, the

Foel Valve Tower alongside Caban Coch reservoir of the Elan Valley scheme in Powys; water from the tower flows by gravity 118 km to Birmingham. The Garreg Ddu viaduct conceals a submerged dam to ensure the water level is always maintained.

Vyrnwy Dam was a pioneer among masonry dams: it was the first to have under-drains, the first to be designed on reasonably scientific principles and the first high masonry dam (26 metres). At the time, it impounded the largest artificial reservoir in Europe. In the words of the *Illustrated London News*, the creation of this new lake was a process of artificial restoration, replacing a lake that had once been cut by a glacier. The masonry dam 'realize[d] the original intention of Nature, making it a lake after all'.[4] The dam was originally to have been made of earth, and indeed the Parliamentary Act of 1880 approving the scheme specified an earth embankment. However a cloudburst in the catchment area as the detailed drawings were being prepared inspired the change to a masonry dam, its crest acting as a weir and thus dispensing with a separate spillway. The dam itself is 335 metres long and is constructed of irregular stone blocks weighing up to 10 tons each bedded with cement mortar and then faced in stone. This tradition of gravity dam design aimed to resist the pressure of the impounded water to move or tip over the dam. Such massive structures have more substantial profiles than their contemporaries in order to both ensure and give the impression of absolute safety. Such safety margins were achieved at a price, however, and led to the design of more economical arch or buttress dams, as we shall see. The draw-off or 'straining tower' (so called because it included a copper gauze mesh to remove suspended matter before transmission to Liverpool) is said to be in the style of a Rhine castle. Built of concrete with stone facing, the 50-metre-high tower was pre-stressed – another innovation at the time.

The Vyrnwy reservoir submerged the village of Llanwyddin, which comprised 40 or 50 cottages, a church and cemetery, a village inn and Eunant Hall. Liverpool Corporation built a new church and moved the remains of the dead to the new site. The reservoir was the subject of Emlyn Williams's 1949 film *Last Days of Dolwyn*, in

which he had the vicar entreating the Borough Engineer not to do 'more harm than you have to'.[5]

Rather than let the dams speak for themselves, celebration of their engineers' or clients' achievements in aesthetic and even symbolic terms came naturally to their Victorian creators. Were they also advertising their triumphs? It would be some years before the architect Louis Sullivan's dictum 'Form follows function' could be applied to dams.

Apart from their functions, which are varied, dams convey a variety of symbolic meanings. In this respect they differ from other engineering structures or edifices – they can be read in many ways. The terms that come to mind are *power, strength, achievement, domination* – not all of them complimentary! – as well as *civilization*, both in general terms as a level of cultural development and encapsulated specifically by the phrase 'hydraulic civilization'. As a starting point for cultural development we need look no further than the Khadjoo diversion dam in the city of Isfahan in Iran. Iran has a history of water management dating to 700 BC, when *qanat*s (horizontal wells) were introduced from Armenia. They served as a most important part of irrigation and are still used to this day. Construction of the Amir Dam at Shiraz started 1000 years ago and was a typical multi-functional structure, being a mill, a dam and a bridge. During the Safavid era, water engineering developed

Blocks of stone being lowered into place by steam-driven cranes in 1888 for the masonry dam closing Lake Vyrnwy, Powys.

Vyrnwy Tower, from where water is transmitted to Liverpool via 110 km of aqueduct and pipeline.

significantly, and many diversion and storage dams were built.[6] The Khadjoo, constructed in the 1650s under Shah Abbas II, doubles as a bridge and was described by Lord Curzon in 1892 as the most beautiful dam in the entire world.[7] It only holds back 3 metres of river head but is 180 metres long. Iran has stayed at the forefront of dam building, and has demonstrated its pride in its achievements by illustrations on 'First Day Covers'.

The term 'hydraulic civilizations' was first used by Karl Wittfogel in 1957.[8] Such civilizations were made possible by engineering skills which protected land from floods and irrigated crops. The Mesopotamians in the valleys of the Tigris and the Euphrates provide one example; the Egyptians on the Nile were another. Wittfogel maintained that their society was dependent on their ability to organize and control the labour force necessary to build and maintain canals and embankments. In other words, an autocratic government was essential.

Domination was therefore the watchword – of citizens as well as

First Day Cover showing the Sepid Rood Dam, Iran.

of nature. King Parakrama and his 'sea' at Polonnaruwa in Sri Lanka was an excellent example of such an arrangement. Built in the twelfth century, the Parakrama Samudra Dam – at 15 metres high and with a crest 13.6 kilometres long – used more fill than any other dam in the world until the construction of the Gatun Dam for the Panama Canal in 1912. It is estimated that it would have taken some 50,000 man-years to build – so for a construction period of five years, a workforce of 10,000 labourers was required.

So we have sovereignty, over the indigenous population and over other states, but what of control of nature?

The US Bureau of Reclamation, created in 1902 by President Theodore Roosevelt, concentrated on the taming of rivers, and one of its first tasks was to harness the Colorado. While the Hoover Dam was intended to control flooding and provide hydroelectric power and water supply, the Senate authorisation in 1928 emotively recorded that this 'mighty river, now a source of destruction, is to be curbed

'The most beautiful hydraulic works in the world': the Khadjoo Dam in Isfahan described by Lord Curzon, Viceroy of India.

and put to work in the interests of society'. As Donald Worster put it, 'all wanted to dominate nature . . . and would not be satisfied until the river was under their total domination from headwater to mouth — until the river was dead.'[9] His remark recalls Churchill's about the Nile perishing 'gloriously' and never reaching the sea.

Such statements typify the emotional tension that dams — and rivers — generate. My own view is that rivers should be respected: they have given us life and will continue to do so if cared for and managed. 'Managed' implies a degree of control through engineers' ingenuity and creativity. Dams, though, are the proverbial curate's egg — there are good and bad ones. The worry is that for whatever reason — I would suggest that arrogance plays a part — engineers, clients or nations have often refused to learn from the mistakes of their predecessors. On the positive side of the equation, however, they have often learned from and replicated previous successes, whether in terms of design, construction techniques or appropriateness.

In eighteenth-century England, Lancelot 'Capability' Brown created dams for no other purpose than to change the landscape. Thus at Chatsworth, Stowe and Blenheim, dams were built to create lakes to form new topographical features. One of his most infamous

One of many thousands of ancient irrigation tanks in Sri Lanka (formerly Ceylon), here depicted on a 30c stamp issued between 1938 and 1949.

commissions was for Lord Milton in 1774 who regarded the village of Milton Abbas as a blot on his landscape when viewed from his new mansion. Milton demolished the village of some 500 inhabitants and had it rebuilt to Brown's design in an adjacent valley, out of sight. Milton bought the leases of the houses and most of the villagers 'surrendered without a fuss, but others resisted, including a lawyer named Harrison'.[10] So Milton had the sluice gates of the Abbot's pond opened, flooding Harrison's house.

Sometimes dams can represent struggles between adjacent nation-states. The creation of Pakistan in 1947 put the headwaters of the Indus in India but the main river in Pakistan. This problem was solved by the World Bank, who allocated the waters of three tributaries to India and the rest of the basin to Pakistan. The 2,500-metre-long Mangla embankment dam on the Indus basin is a symbol of Pakistan's determination to develop her water and power resources to meet the needs of a growing population. It forms part of the World Bank's solution arrived at when the long, drawn-out dispute between India and Pakistan regarding their respective riparian rights was resolved with the signing of the Indus Waters Treaty. The treaty, signed in 1960, took nine years of negotiation; 'It marked the end of a water dispute which appeared at one time not only insoluble but brought the two countries almost to the brink of war'.[11] In 1963 India created the 226-metre-high Bhakra gravity dam on one of its allocated tributaries.

Similarly, co-operation was required between Sudan and Egypt for the management and exploitation of the Nile. The river has its headwaters in Ethiopia and Sudan but for its last 2,400 kilometres it flows through Egypt. The Sennar Dam, built in 1925 on the Blue Nile for Sudan, required arrangements with Egypt to allow the continued efficient use of the Aswan and Assiut dams. Then the Gebel Anlia Dam on the White Nile was built in Sudan on behalf of Egypt

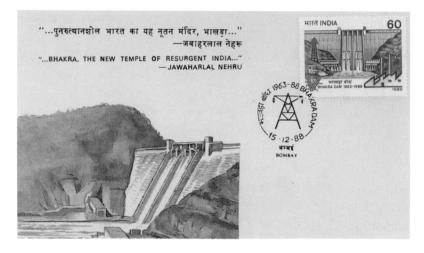

'Bhakra Dam – The New Temple of Resurgent India': Jawaharlal Nehru. First Day Cover, 1963.

to supplement the Aswan Dam. As we shall see, a new agreement between Sudan and Egypt to replace the 1929 Nile Waters Agreement had to be drawn up in 1957 for the new Aswan High Dam funded by the Soviet Union. This resulted in Sudan receiving £15 million compensation as well as four times as much water as before, albeit only a quarter of Egypt's share. There have been several Nile agreements since in the Nile basin.

Such dams are symbols of social upheaval – the Aswan High Dam required 150,000 people to be resettled. This figure is dwarfed, however, by the number being relocated in the construction of the Three Gorges Dam! Although the Three Gorges is being promoted as saving people from annual floods as well as generating much needed power, Dai Qing sees it as an icon of superpower status and national prestige.[12]

The construction of the High Dam at Aswan was a symbol of Russian influence (and power) in Africa and of Soviet association with liberation and anti-colonialism.[13] In 1958, when President Kwame Nkrumah of Ghana determined to build the Akosombo Dam as a symbol of Ghana's arrival in the modern world around which the new country could unite, the US President Dwight Eisenhower couldn't allow the USSR to extend its African power base any further and persuaded the Kaiser Corporation of America to undertake the project. The site on the River Volta had been surveyed by Sir Albert Kitson of the British Gold Coast Geological Survey as early as 1915; Kitson dreamed of creating a dam to provide hydroelectricity for smelting aluminium from a recently discovered deposit of bauxite.

Kitson's plans went nowhere until the 1940s, when they were resurrected by the British, who envisaged a Volta River Authority modelled on the American Tennessee Valley Authority (TVA) to propel Ghana into the Industrial Age. This plan was inaugurated in 1966 but was something of a white elephant, with Kaiser importing their own bauxite and using 50 per cent of the power generated themselves. Resettlement, disease, silting behind the dam and coastal erosion (due to reduced material deposited by the Volta at its mouth) are the legacies. Nevertheless, the dam was rebuilt in 1991 and features on Ghanaian phone cards.

The TVA was also set up to 'save' people. Introduced by President Franklin Roosevelt in 1933 as part of his New Deal to regenerate the

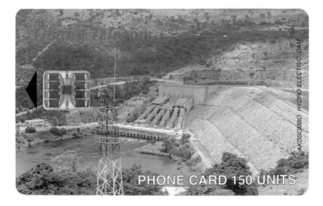

Phone card from Ghana showing the Akosombo Dam.

American South, it comprised a number of multi-purpose dams requiring co-operation between several different states for their mutual benefit. Roosevelt's ambition was to turn John Steinbeck's 'Grapes of Wrath' into Grapes of Wealth by the creation of large dams in the West as well as the South. In many respects the TVA and the California and Colorado schemes represent modern hydraulic civilizations with their need for vast resources and organization to achieve 'sustainable' communities in inhospitable environments. As the Republican President Calvin Coolidge (who approved the Hoover Dam) had said, 'the chief business of the American people is business.'[14]

As we shall see, dams also symbolize fear – of collapse, of attack, of destruction. We will also discover the anger they have generated – particularly since the second half of the twentieth century – though initially, for many, they instilled a sense of pride. This is evidenced by the proliferation of postcards, first-day covers and advertisements inspired by them, as well as the usual souvenirs. The fact that *Life* magazine chose as its first cover in 1936 a striking image of Fort Peck Dam in Montana, celebrated again some 50 years later by the US Postal Service, speaks volumes.

But what do dams actually do? Dams can be multi-purpose, but generally they are initiated to solve a single problem.

Irrigation

The first dams – the essence of hydraulic civilisations – were built for irrigation. In India 'large tanks employing sophisticated methods of water control, were a feature of life. In southern India a dense patchwork of small, independent village tanks and irrigation systems was overlain by a network of great reservoirs, to feed imperial cities, armies and parks.'[15] Initially at least, the British admired these systems and renovated the major ancient waterworks (while ignoring

the village tanks). The earlier schemes were essentially diversion dams, but in the nineteenth century, storage dams — which were more elaborate and therefore expensive — were built. As early as 1808, there had been a plan for an irrigation scheme on the River Periyar for Madurai, but it took another 60 years before Professor W.J.M. Rankine at Glasgow was consulted on the form of dam required; it was eventually built in 1897.

Towards the end of the nineteenth century, slender arch dams for irrigation were built in North America and Australia. One of the boldest of all, the Bear Valley Dam in California designed by Frank E. Brown, has been described as 'more daring than the contemporary state of knowledge really warranted'.[16] It was built in 1884 to impound irrigation water at over 2,000 metres above sea level in the San Bernardino Mountains, 130 kilometres east of Los Angeles.

The site was particularly remote so, faced with the need to get men, equipment and materials over more than a hundred kilometres of mountain and desert roads, Brown had an incentive to build as economically as he could — which meant as thin a dam as he dared. It was built of a rubble masonry core set in Portland-cement mortar

Life magazine's first edition cover featured a photograph of Fort Peck Dam, Montana, by Margaret Bourke-White. It was reproduced 50 years later on the 32c postage stamp to 'celebrate the century' of the US Postal Service.

faced with rough-cut masonry blocks. The masonry was laid from rafts floating on the rising reservoir. But the dam's boldness lay in the fact that at 20 metres high and 90 metres long it was less than 1 metre thick at its crest and just over 2 metres near the base.

People were always concerned about the safety of the Bear Valley Dam, and it was thought that a severe flood would overload it. However, it stood for 26 years before being replaced by a multiple-arch dam in 1910, in response to the need for more water for the citrus groves whose creation had been made possible by the original dam. The Bear Valley Dam still stands beneath the water of the new reservoir. The new dam, designed by John Eastwood (whom we shall meet again), was 28 metres high but held three times as much water in its reservoir as the original.

Frank Brown went on to design an irrigation dam for San Diego on the Sweetwater River – initially to the same bold, slim design – but

Periyar Dam, Kerala, India built in 1897 to provide irrigation for the adjacent state of Tamil Nadu.

its promoters lost their nerve, and handed the completion to James Schuyler; when completed in 1888 it was more substantial than originally intended: at 30 metres tall it was nearly 4 metres thick at its crest. It was carefully made of locally quarried porphyry – a very heavy stone – and imported English and German cement. The quality of its design and construction was severely tested in 1895 when heavy rain submerged the crest to a depth of 0.5 metres for two days.

The farmers of California always seem to be desperate for water, and the tallest embankment dam in the world at the time was built in 1886 on the Otay Creek 30 kilometres south-east of San Diego. This was an extraordinary design, having a steel plate at its core against which were piled loose rocks sloping on both the air and the water faces. It was 49 metres high and 172 metres long but was washed away by overtopping by a flood in 1916. (The later Upper Otay Dam, constructed between 1899 and 1900, was another first in the world of dam building, being of reinforced concrete.)

While the Nile had been managed for centuries for irrigation and the fertility it brought with it in its silt, the first dam ever built across its main stream was constructed in 1902. Described by Norman

Sweetwater Dam, California, in 1910. Originally designed by Frank E. Brown in 1888, it withstood the flood of 1895 when its crest was submerged for two days.

Smith as 'one of the finest dam building achievements of all time',[17] it was an extraordinary 2 kilometres long and 39 metres tall and built of locally quarried granite. It had 180 sluices which controlled the river and fed it to the Assiut barrage some 400 kilometres downstream which then diverted the rich, silty water to the fields.

The original plans for the Aswan-Assiut were drawn up by Sir William Willcocks, who spent three years in Egypt surveying the Nile. This dam was so successful that its height was raised in 1912 and again in 1933 to a total of 38 metres.

Navigation

One of the earliest dams built for navigation before the modern era was the Saint-Ferreol, constructed in 1675 by Pierre-Paul Riquet for the Canal du Midi in France. There had been previous plans to link the Atlantic with the Mediterranean, but they had foundered on the problem of getting sufficient water to the proposed canal summit. Riquet hit on the idea to dam the River Laudot to collect

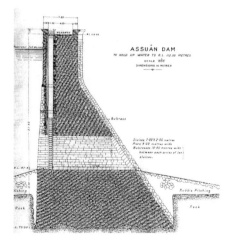

Sir William Willcocks's section of the 1902 Aswan (Assuân) Dam. 'At the time of designing the dam, I intended that . . . it could be raised 6 metres in height.'

the winter run-off from the Montagne Noire to supply the canal. His dam had a central masonry wall and two revetment walls to contain an earth core; the three walls all penetrated to the bedrock to a depth of between 2 and 3 metres. The dam is 786 metres long and has a maximum height of 32 metres – at the time of its construction it was the largest dam in the world.

Some of the earliest engineered dams in Britain were built for the canal boom in the eighteenth century. Dams for navigation were

The completed first Aswan Dam in 1902.

A postcard of the Temple of Isis at Philae, submerged by the second Aswan Dam.

not new; indeed one of the oldest surviving earth dams in England was built in 1189 by Godfrey de Lucy, Bishop of Winchester. Having decided to make the Itchen navigable from Southampton to Alresford in Hampshire, he built a dam 6 metres high and 76 metres long at Alresford.

Some of the most famous British engineers of the 1700s were responsible for building dams, including Thomas Telford, John Rennie and William Jessop. Initially river and contour canal navigation required little extra water supply, but when commercial interests demanded cross-country connections, summit-level supplies were required.

Rennie designed the 11-metre-high Rudyard Embankment Dam in 1797 for the Trent and Mersey Canal. He prescribed a 'puddle clay' core 1.8 metres thick at the top and 3.7 metres wide at its base, a specification that was to apply for more than a hundred years. This dam also had a curved overflow crest to increase its discharge capacity. The slope of the embankment was 1:2 on the downstream face and 1:1.7 on the upstream one. The properties of puddle clay had been demonstrated to a Parliamentary Committee by James

Alresford reservoir, Hampshire, built in 1189. A road now crosses the dam and the water irrigates watercress beds downstream.

Brindley in 1762 when he had 'caused a mass of clay to be brought into the Committee Room . . . he worked up the clay with water to imitate the process of puddling and . . . filled it with water, which was held without a particle of leakage'.[18]

A navigation dam with a chequered history was built in 1823 to supply the Bude Canal in Cornwall. The grand plan was to link the English and Bristol Channels. The Canal was only ever partly built and fell into decline; the local council bought the Tamar Lake in 1902 to supply Bude with drinking water. In 1973 the North Devon Water Board commissioned Rofe, Kennard and Lapworth as consulting engineers to rebuild the Tamar Dam and provide an additional reservoir upstream. Today, the Tamar Lakes form a vital component of South West Water's supply system.

In Canada, the Rideau Canal linking Ottawa with Kingston on Lake Ontario was constructed between 1826 and 1832 by a team of British Royal Engineers led by Lieut-Col. John By. This required a total of 52 dams, some of which were earth embankments and a few of which were masonry. The biggest was Jones Falls. In 1795, a Pennsylvania wheelwright, Oliver Evans, published his *Young Mill-Wright and Miller's Guide*. Apart from describing types of timber dams, he also wrote about masonry dams, recommending that they be curved in plan. John By built the 19-metre-high dam on the Rideau Canal with just such a curvature and with a central angle at the crest of 115 degrees. This was probably one of the Royal Engineers' last efforts in North America, although they carried on their work in India and elsewhere. By's dam on the Rideau Canal was the first arched dam in North America, and at the time it was built, in 1832, it was also the tallest. The masonry blocks were laid in vertical courses in order to more readily facilitate the curvature. It is still working as a canal reservoir but now also generates electricity.

A dam which held the world record in terms of embankment volume at the time of its construction is the Gatun Dam for the Panama Canal, completed in 1912. It holds back the Chagres River and created the 420 sq km Gatun Lake, thus providing sufficient draught for navigation. Apart from controlling the level of the lake, the Gatun Dam also provides electrical power for the Canal.

Water Supply

The demands of the Industrial Revolution led to an increased provision of water for industry as well as for human consumption. Almost without exception, reservoirs were impounded in Britain by embankment dams, the design and construction of which were based on the empirical knowledge and experience gained through the construction of ornamental and navigation dams. The first important water-supply structure was the 21-metre-high, 150-metre-long Glencorse Dam, built between 1819 and 1822 to compensate mill owners and landowners for water diverted to the city of Edinburgh. The engineer was Thomas Telford; he was assisted by James Jardine. John Rennie acted for the landowners and millers. Glencorse had the same puddle-clay core as Rudyard and followed the principles laid down there.

John Smeaton had proposed the use of springs for water supply to the south of Edinburgh in the Pentland Hills earlier in the eighteenth century. Following a water shortage in 1810, Telford suggested using one of these, the Crawley Spring, but judged correctly that the millers and landowners would object to its diversion. He solved the problem with a reservoir on the Glencorse Burn from which compensation water could be directed downstream for the use of these riparian owners. Even with Rennie's support, the owners were not convinced, and it took a further shortage in 1818 to lead to action.

The specification for Glencorse was endorsed by the three engineers. It was a difficult construction with Telford insisting that the puddle-clay core be taken down to bedrock – this was 'not to be avoided, perfect safety is absolutely necessary'.[19] The puddle trench had to be taken 38 metres below the crest before reaching sound rock beneath the river-bed; the core was 18 metres wide at ground level. That the dam still serves Edinburgh's water-supply needs is a testament to the pedigree of its joint designers. Its height was increased in 1848, and by the mid-nineteenth century five more earth dams were built on the same pattern for the city.

In 1804 in India, several years before these famous British engineers were following their rather staid if safe principles, the Mir Alam Dam was designed for the water supply of Hyderabad. There is confusion about who the designer was, and, while the Hyderabad Water Works maintain that it was a French engineer, Henry Russell, serving in the Madras Engineering Corps, others state that it was Lieut. Samuel Ranott. This dam is of a quite remarkable design (not replicated for another 120 years until the Coolidge Dam in Arizona) consisting of 21

Glencorse Dam, Edinburgh. One of Telford's few dams, it was completed in 1822.

semi-circular vertical arches about 12 metres high. Nicholas Schnitter described it as 'One of the rare, true strokes of genius'.[20]

The first multiple-arch dam in the world, the Mir Alam is some 1,300 metres long in the form of a curve with the overflow discharged partially through a spillway at one end while the rest pours over the crest. In 200 years this has not damaged the masonry and mortar, nor has it undermined the foundations. The dam was renovated in 1980.

Received wisdom was challenged elsewhere in the world. For example, the evidence of developments in New South Wales was made available when L.A.B. Wade presented a paper in March 1909 to a meeting of the Institution of Civil Engineers in London entitled 'Concrete and Masonry Dam Construction in New South Wales'. All of these dams were extremely slender and caused consternation especially because gravity dams with heavy profiles (such as that at Vyrnwy) were more usual in Europe. Sir Alexander Binnie professed that the Australian dam profiles produced a 'blood-curdling sensation'; others warned that Australian dam engineers had taken dam-building to a dangerous point.[21] The thinnest, the Medlow arch

One of the 21 semi-circular arches of the Mir Alam Dam, Hyderabad, 1804, 'one of the rare, true strokes of genius'.

dam, was less than a metre thick at its crest and less than 3 metres thick at its base. At 20 metres high, this was a surprising proportion. However, they were all built, were all performing satisfactorily and safely, and were clearly a success. Cost was the driving force behind the design – thin profiles required less material.

The US was slow at first to build water-supply dams, but a number had been completed by 1850. The most important and biggest one was that constructed between 1837 and 1842 across the Croton River north of New York, having been proposed by John B. Jervis in 1835. New York's demands were more than could be supplied from local springs and wells, and Jervis looked further afield. The Croton is a tributary of the Hudson River, from where water was brought to New York by a 68-kilometre brick aqueduct. Initially the dam was to be partially earth embankment, but it was washed away during construction in 1841 and so was completed as a masonry dam, creating an 'artificial' rock foundation in the process. When completed, the Croton Dam was 120 metres long and 15 metres high with its water

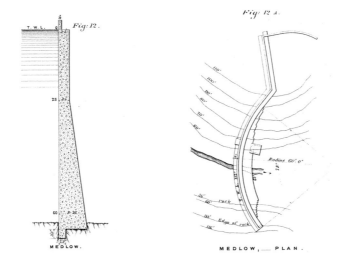

Profiles of thin arch dams from New South Wales presented to the Institution of Civil Engineers in London in 1909 – 'a blood-curdling sensation'.

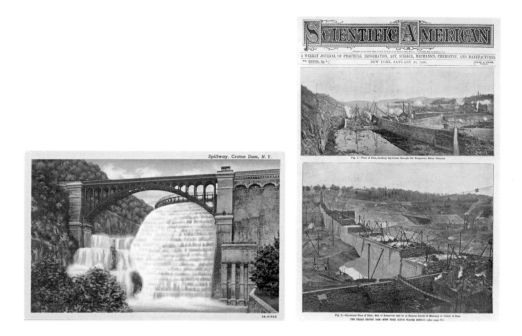

face protected by an earth bank at a gradient of 1:5. This in turn was protected by stone, and the overflow was allowed to discharge over the central 60 metres of the dam. There was a downstream wooden apron to prevent the whole structure being undermined. As a further safety measure, a small timber dam was built a little way downstream which flooded the space between itself and the main dam — keeping the foundations saturated and breaking the force of water overflow.

The Croton Dam served New York for some 50 years but then 'suffered the supreme indignity'.[22] Between 1892 and 1906 a new and much bigger structure, the New Croton Dam, was built 5.2 kilometres downstream, submerging the original dam in its reservoir. The new dam was 91 metres high and 329 metres long. *Scientific American* described it as being

faced with a very handsome, light-coloured granite, which will have the appearance of marble, and with the parapet and ornamental finish which

The New Croton Dam on the Hudson River, New York, built in 1906 for New York City's water supply.

'The Great Croton Dam, New York City's water supply'.

it is intended to give the crest, the finished structure will have an exceedingly handsome and imposing appearance . . . the old Croton dam . . . will be buried below the surface of a beautiful lake eight square miles in extent which will henceforth form not the least attractive feature of this most attractive country.[23]

Evidence indeed that dams and their reservoirs have been regarded by some as contributing to the landscape.

Hydropower

Hydropower 'is among the most significant technological consequences of the whole of nineteenth century science and engineering'.[24] The water turbine was the natural successor to the water wheel, but in its mode of operation it was a fundamentally new idea; with the development of electromagnetism it was possible to produce power from water at one place and then transmit it to a city hundreds of kilometres away.

In order to drive a water turbine, a head of water is required, and early hydroelectric installations made use of natural differences in water level. One such was the Niagara Falls project built in the 1890s to supply electricity to Buffalo more than 30 kilometres away. Such sites do not always occur naturally, and it was inevitable that dams would be required for future development. As Norman Smith put it,

Three separate technologies − those concerning dams, water turbines and electric generators − experienced a marriage towards the end of the nineteenth century. It is one of the supreme examples of seemingly diverse branches of engineering coming together to found a new branch of the subject.[25]

Initially dams were used for hydroelectric installations as part of run-of-river schemes – i.e. they raised the level of the river but did not create any significant storage. The first example of such an arrangement was built in 1882 on the Fox River at Appleton, Wisconsin. The Colorado River was dammed for hydroelectricity at Austin, Texas in 1893, as we shall see. It was in the western US that conditions were especially favourable to the development of hydropower schemes: in the mountains, the rapid fall of the rivers favoured the establishment of high heads of water. This has led to what Eva Jakobsson has termed the 'Industrialization of Rivers'.[26]

Other countries which capitalized on their topography to generate electricity were Norway and Switzerland, where today 100 per cent of their energy is derived from hydroelectricity. Tyssedal in the Sørfjorden near Bergen was one of the pioneer sites in the development of hydroelectric power in Norway. The power station built

Ringedals curved gravity dam in Norway, built in 1918.

between 1906 and 1918 is supplied by the Ringedals reservoir in the valley of Skjeggedal created by a curved-concrete gravity dam, 521 metres long and 35 metres high, built between 1912 and 1918. The Ringedals Dam, one of the biggest in Scandinavia when it was built, leaked from the beginning, and it was decided in 1928 to

Pipes from the Ringedals reservoir to Tyssedal Power Station on Sørfjorden, Norway.

place a watertight diaphragm made of reinforced concrete 2 metres from the upstream face of the existing structure.

In Britain, the government set up the Water Power Resources Committee after the First World War to investigate the opportunities for hydropower. It concluded that the greatest potential lay in Scotland. By this time the Kinlochleven scheme, Britain's first large-scale hydropower project, had been in operation for ten years. Further schemes were approved, but it was to be another ten years before they came to fruition. However, by the late 1930s, Lochaber, Grampian, Devon and Galloway were fully operational. These were often natural lochs whose levels were raised by the construction of dams with the water then piped to generating stations. After some resistance to further developments by riparian owners, local authorities and sporting interests, the needs of the Second World War inspired the setting up of the North of Scotland Hydro-Electric Board in 1943.

However, because such schemes were often difficult to justify on economic grounds and were in remote locations, radical departures

The Tyssedal Power Station, 1918.

from accepted practice were required to economize on time, labour or materials – or on the sheer challenge of building in such places. The dam at Loch Sloy was the first of a number of concrete buttress dams. This was more than 50 metres high and of the type known as 'diamond-headed'. Even more revolutionary was the Allt-na-Lairige Dam at 20 metres high and 400 metres long: it used only 60 per cent of the concrete of conventional gravity dams by pre-stressing with iron rods and was the first of its kind in the world. This dam was typical of the 'originality, variety and technical interest of Britain's hydro-electric dams'.[27] The principal dam on the Afon Prysor, part of the Maentwrog scheme of the North Wales Power Company completed in 1928 and impounding Lake Trawsfynydd, was the first large concrete arch dam in Britain. (It was replaced in 1991 when a new concrete gravity dam, 40 metres high, was built by Nuclear Electric to provide cooling water for a nuclear power station.)

However, these were not the first proposals for hydropower in Britain. In 1850 a remarkable scheme had been proposed for a tidal power barrage across the Severn Estuary. These plans were stillborn,

Loch Sloy 'diamond head' concrete buttress dam for the North of Scotland Hydro-Electric Board, built in 1950.

but attempts at revival have been made periodically, in 1989 by the Severn Tidal Power Group and, most recently, by the Welsh Assembly and private developers in 2006. Hydropower continues to be developed in the Highlands: in 2005 Scottish & Southern Energy completed a 110-metre-long concrete dam at Kingairloch (helicopters had to be used to bring concrete to the remote site), and at Glendoe they built a 35-metre-high rock-fill dam – all as part of the Scottish Climate Change Programme to generate electricity from renewable sources.

A similar scheme to that proposed for the Severn has been operating on the estuary of La Rance River in Brittany since 1967. First conceived in 1921, it was the first and is still the biggest tidal power plant in the world: the barrage itself is 750 metres long, with the turbines utilizing the tide and the river in turn. The plant has now paid for itself and the electricity generated is two-thirds the cost of nuclear.

The largest scheme built just for hydropower is the 12,600 MW Itaipu Dam on the Brazil / Paraguay border – a double-buttress dam 196 metres high and a total of 7.75 kilometres long, constructed in 1983 on the Rio Parana, the second-biggest river in South America. It provides electricity to Rio de Janeiro and São Paulo and makes Paraguay the largest exporter of electricity in the world; in accordance with the Itaipu Treaty of 1974, Paraguay uses what electricity it needs from the scheme and then sells its surplus to Brazil.

Severn Tidal Barrage, 1850. Painting by Thomas Fulljames, who proposed a 1.5km-long barrage with 20 arches carrying a road on the lower level and a railway on the upper level, from Aust in Gloucestershire to Beachley in Monmouthshire.

This dam took 40,000 workers seven years to build, thus solving Brazil's energy problem — with insufficient oil and gas and without the ability to import, the country turned to hydropower. The turbines produce enough electricity in a year to satisfy the demands of a city three times the size of London. The dam cost the loss of 600 square kilometres of Brazilian farmland and 470 of Paraguay's rainforest; 8,500 homes and farms had to be relocated. Work started in 1975, and a new town was built to house the labour force, which came from all over Brazil. The concrete dam wall is hollow to save the cost of concrete — it uses 25 per cent less concrete than a solid-gravity dam — and comprises eighteen buttresses.[28] In the tropical heat, the concrete had to be cooled for pouring to 7 degrees C using two refrigeration plants, the equivalent of 50,000 domestic freezers. The first electricity was generated in 1984 and it worked well until

Itaipu Dam on the Parana River between Paraguay and Brazil, described by *Popular Mechanics* as one of the 'Seven Wonders of the Modern World'. The volume of rock excavated was more than eight times that of the Channel Tunnel between France and Britain.

January 2002, when the power lines to Rio, 1,000 kilometres away, could no longer cope – halting lifts and trains and causing traffic to stop at permanently red lights. (The power lines have since been upgraded). The American magazine *Popular Mechanics* claimed the 'workers had re-enacted the labours of Hercules as they shifted the course of the seventh biggest river in the world'.[29]

Flood Control

The need for flood-control schemes has grown with the rapidly growing world population. They are needed in the developing world to defend newly established populations but were initiated in the intensively crowded conditions of Europe. An early application of gravity-dam theory was implemented at Saint-Etienne in eastern France on the River Furens in 1861, when a 60-metre-high, 250-metre-long curved-masonry dam was built to protect the town.

In the twentieth century, schemes were developed to protect Los Angeles (San Gabriel, 1939) and Seattle (Mud Mountain, 1948), both more than 120-metre-tall embankment dams. However, if you live

A 1983 Brazilian First Day Cover showing the Itaipu Dam.

in what the rest of the world calls the Low Countries, flood protection comes as standard. A third of Holland lies below sea level; during a previous period of climate change, at the end of the Ice Age, as the polar ice and glaciers melted, Holland was inundated. By the nineteenth century, 10,000 windmills were needed to pump water from farmland. Dykes keep out the ravages of North Sea storm surges, as well as reclaiming land for their tulips. The most significant is the Zuiderzee, built in the 1930s and creating 200,000 hectares of freshwater and a similar area of agricultural land.

Original plans for the works date back to 1667, when Hendric Stevin proposed damming the Zuiderzee, but they were not feasible at that time. In 1891 an engineer, Cornelis Lely, put forward a plan to create four new polders, or areas of new land. Opposition came from fishermen and people in coastal areas. However, Lely became Minister of Transport and Public Works in 1913, and when dykes burst and thousands of lives were lost in 1916 the impetus finally was there for the Zuiderzee Act of 1918 and for work to begin. The main dam, the Afsluitdijk (closure-dyke) was started in 1927. This was to have a length of 32 kilometres, a width of 90 metres and a height above sea level of 7.3 metres. Most of the dam was built in relatively shallow water by dredging clay from the bottom of the Zuiderzee and depositing it in two parallel lines; the space between them was then filled with sand. The underwater sections were willow mattresses weighted down by rocks, all placed by hand. Closure was achieved on 28 May 1932. This created the Ijsselmeer, or Lake Ijssel. Within the lake, the land was reclaimed by building an encircling dyke and then pumping out the water. The third polder to be drained played an important role for the Dutch Resistance in the Second World War since it provided useful hiding places. The retreating Germans blew up the dyke of the Weieringermeer in April 1945, thus submerging the polder;

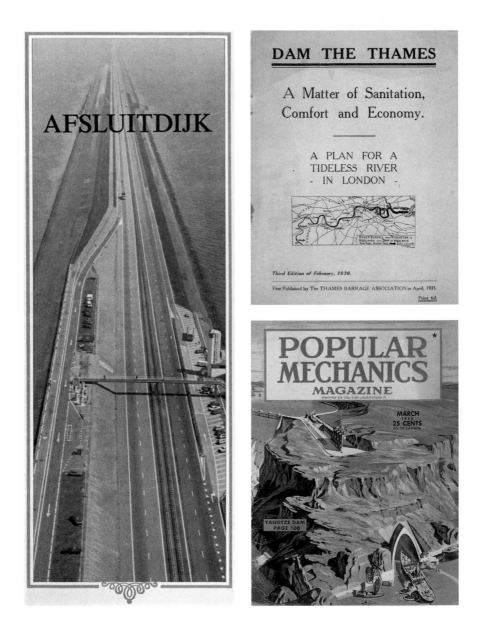

The Afsluitdijk or 'closure dike' in the north of the Netherlands. Completed in 1937, it turned the salt water Zuiderzee, an inlet of the North Sea, into a freshwater lake.

The 1935 plan to dam the Thames proposed by the Thames Barrage Association.

The Yangtze Dam as anticipated in 1946, from the front cover of *Popular Mechanics Magazine*.

reconstruction was complete, however, by the end of the year. The area of Flevoland, the last polder of 1,000 square kilometres, was completed after the war and is now Almere, the fastest-growing city in the Netherlands. There are 25 sluices in all to discharge water from the Ijsselmeer together with locks for shipping.

Following the 1953 floods along the North Sea coasts, the Delta Plan came into being. Further links were built along the coast but could not be permanent since this would have destroyed the fishing industry, so steel sluice gates were installed that can be raised when high tides are forecast. There are 62 sluice gates with piers 15 storeys high. The risk to the land behind the largest sea barrier in the world is now 1:4,000 years. However, with the climate changing again, the plan has been revised, and in extreme storm and sea-surge events land (and villages) will be temporarily flooded in order that most of the country can remain protected. With engineering (and Dutch) ingenuity, homes are now being built on pontoons which can rise with the rising waters.

Following the Dutch example, proposals were put forward in 1935 for a scheme to protect London. A dam at London Bridge had been proposed in 1858 but could not reasonably be implemented owing to the sewage discharges to the Thames at the time: tides were still needed to remove the sewage. However, in the 1870s, Bazalgette's 135 kilometres of intercepting sewers took London's sewage downstream to Barking and Crossness. By the 1930s, with river traffic of more than 7,000 ships a year using London's docks, a scheme was proposed by the Thames Barrage Association. A barrage was proposed to be located at Woolwich, for navigation as well as for flood defence. One other advantage listed by the Association was the enhancement of value of riverside property 'business premises by increased accessibility, private premises by disappearance of mudflats, smells and decaying matter'.[30]

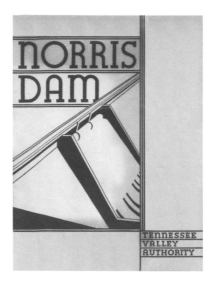

It was to take another 40 years before the Thames 'Barrage' was completed – by which time the docks had left London. Rising tides and sea level were now seen as a real threat. The threat has multiplied since then, with climate change threatening to overwhelm the Barrier.

A scheme that is at last coming to fruition is the Three Gorges on the Yangtze River in China. Dams have been built on this, the third-largest river in the world since AD 190 for irrigation as well as for flood control upstream of Shanghai.

In the twentieth century, the Yangtze (Chang) floodwaters drowned a total of 300,000 people and left millions homeless. The idea of dams at the Three Gorges upstream of Wuhan was first proposed in the 1920s. In the 1940s the US Bureau of Reclamation co-operated with the Chinese to develop plans for the dam sites. The main dam proposed at Ichang would have used twice as much concrete as Grand Coulee, have been taller than the Hoover Dam and have created a lake more than 600 kilometres long.

The Norris Dam, east Tennessee, 1936. The first dam of the TVA (Tennessee Valley Authority) – a concrete gravity dam designed in the modernist style.

Soviet dam builders took over in the 1950s until political differences led to them being dismissed. Further floods, drowning 30,000 people in 1954, prompted Chairman Mao to continue the plans. The Cultural Revolution postponed the scheme until, in the 1970s, Premier Deng Xiaopeng succeeded in tabling it in the 1981–5 Five-Year Plan. The help of American and Canadian engineers was enlisted. Why China needed help is something of a mystery, however, since the country has been the most prolific dam builder the world has ever seen, constructing more than 20,000 large dams in the latter half of the twentieth century (and peaking at more than a thousand new dams per year in the 1970s). In 1992 the project was approved by the National People's Congress, and work started on a dam that was to occupy 40,000 people for sixteen years. The scheme will protect 10 million people downstream, generate electricity and improve navigation. The costs of the 1998 floods alone will be recouped by the capital costs. The 200-metre-high, 2-kilometre-long dam was completed in 2004 and the lake began to fill, and the river called the Great Dragon began to be tamed. (The highest water level will be reached in 2009.) With the economic boom town Shanghai as the dragon's head, the dam 'is a symbol of technological achievement, China's arrival and the debt owed to the community'.[31] It will also generate electricity equivalent to the output of a dozen nuclear power stations.

However, for all the environmental benefits there is, inevitably, a downside. Apart from the need to resettle 1.4 million people, the waste from the city of Chongqing, 400 kilometres upstream, continues to discharge into the river that has become a lake. Rehousing farmers displaced by the rising waters is relatively straightforward, but what are they to farm? Bizarrely, they are being told to dig up their soil and re-lay it on the unfertile hills above the water line. Consultation and public participation are limited in China, with officials answerable to their superiors rather than to the people, so protest has been muted in comparison with other schemes, as we shall see. However, the government (President Hu has a master's degree in water management) took note and delayed final implementation of the scheme to take account of the findings of the WCD. In 2005, the Yangtze Forum was formed, which brought together government departments to develop a common vision for the management and conservation of the river.[32] (The fact that 1.5 million people have been displaced for the modern development of Shanghai helps put The Three Gorges project into perspective.)

Tailings Dams

Perhaps the least romantic dams are those built to contain the waste of industry. Their most common association is with mineral extraction and they can therefore be the most deadly if they fail – the material they hold is often toxic. Tailings are the waste product of the minerals industry and typically consist of ground rock or slurry and this is retained by the dams. Since vast amounts of waste can be produced each day, tailings dams are some of the world's largest structures. The Syncrude Tailings Dam started in 1973 at Fort McMurray, Alberta in Canada, is by volume at 540 million cubic metres, the largest dam in the world. It contains the tailings left over from oil extraction at the site – and as operations continue, so the dam grows.

Multi-Purpose Dams

Having segregated dams according to their primary functions, we need to remember that they are often realized for more than one.

In the latter years of the twentieth century, dams began to be promoted on the basis of a range of applications. The TVA project epitomized the multi-purpose approach, listing among its aims navigation, flood control, hydropower, soil conservation, fishing and public health (for elimination of malaria). Apart from the organization required, the scheme needed the co-ordination of the operation of 32 dams, often with conflicting objectives and functions.

The scheme was about more than technology – 'Instead of regarding their reservoirs merely as reservoirs, the TVA has from the outset, realized their enormous potential for recreation.'[33] Commentators also saw it as a major development in social planning. Julian Huxley, writing in 1943, maintained that the TVA had demonstrated that 'there is no antithesis between democracy and planning and that planning cannot only be reconciled with individual freedom and opportunity, but can be used to enhance and enlarge them.'[34] The project's sometime chairman David Lilienthal was even more enthusiastic: '[The story of the TVA] is an account of how through a modern expression of ancient democratic principles, human energies have been released in furtherance of a common purpose.'[35]

The TVA also represented a breakthrough in terms of dam design. There was collaboration from the beginning between engineers and architects. The dams were consequently designed to 'form a unity with the landscape and enhance its interest and beauty instead of standing out, like so many nineteenth century utilitarian constructions in gross and defiant conflict with the natural environment'. Roland A. Wank, the scheme's chief architect, called the architecture 'one of the instruments of policy in building up a sounder more vital civilisation in the valley'.[36]

One of the most significant multi-purpose dams is the Hoover Dam, built between 1931 and 1935 to control the Colorado River, generate power, and provide water for irrigation and public supply. It was soon followed – and dwarfed in terms of size – by the Grand Coulee on the Columbia River, which added navigation to its palette

of attributes. Pride in these projects was epitomized by their use in advertising everything from automobiles to whiskey, associating their virtues of achievement, reliability and stature with the product in question. The Southern Pacific Railway promoted the 'mighty Roosevelt Dam, that marvellous monument to modern engineering skill' as one of the attractions of its Sunset Route to California and the 'Apache Trail' was built in 1905 to provide access for construction, while the Arizona Orange Association drew on the Tonto Lake formed by the dam to promote its Tonto brand of orange juice.

So dams may be symbols to some – symbols of humanity's temerity and power, the assumption that people can, and should, control the environment – as Alan Ervine has put it, 'the replumbing of the planet'.[37] Hopefully this chapter has demonstrated that, in the right place, dams can be both symbolic and functional. Like many features of contemporary infrastructure, they are forgotten

The Roosevelt Dam, Arizona, a curved-masonry dam completed in 1911 to provide water storage and flood control in the Salt River Valley. In 1996 its height was raised to 107 m and it was encased in concrete.

Solid dam technology associated with a 'solid' American 1960s automobile.

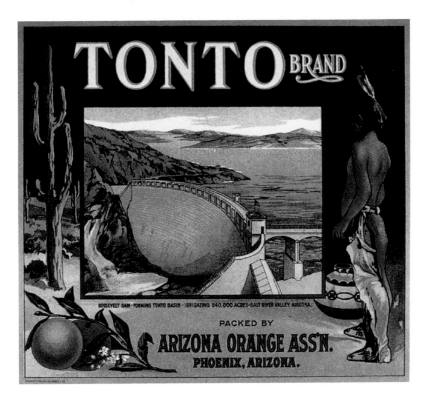

about until either they go wrong or someone plans a new one. We will do well to remember that without them vast numbers of the earth's population would still be walking many kilometres each day for water, would starve, would suffer from disease brought about by inadequate sanitation and would be subject to regular flooding. Without them we would have no chance of arresting global warming. However, much depends on the skills and boldness of their designers and builders, whom we shall meet in the next chapter.

Tonto Brand orange juice advertisement, picturing the Roosevelt Dam.

2 Dam Designers and Builders

The secret fountains to follow up,
Waters withdrawn to restore to the mouth,
And gather the floods as in a cup,
And pour them again at a city's drouth . . .
Rudyard Kipling

Humans may have been building dams for thousands of years, but they were not the first creators of dams on earth – the earth got there first. Retreating glaciers leave behind the rubble of rock, stones and pebbles they have carried. Termed 'moraines', such rubble impounds the glaciated valleys upstream to form lakes. The corrie lakes of Snowdon in North Wales are examples of these, as are the lakes of the English Lake District. In Croatia the lakes in Plitvice National Park are still being formed by deposits of travertine which form dams connecting a series of lakes in this karst limestone region.

And humans are not the only inhabitants of the earth to build dams. The North American and European beaver is an eco-engineer that can build up to 200 kilograms of dam in a day. The longest one measured was 1.5 kilometres. By creating lakes, beavers gain access to tree bark — their favourite food — and provide safe havens for their homes or lodges. They create mosaics of habitats for other wildlife as well as recreational areas in the resulting wet-lands for bird-watching and fishing, and they provide attenuation ponds for melt-water in spring.

The earliest known man-made dam is at Java some 100 kilometres north of Amman in Jordan, built in 3000 BC for water supply. The builders and designers of this structure are long forgotten, but what

Plitvice Lakes, Croatia, a UNESCO World Heritage Site.

do we know of the dam builders of the modern era? In Samuel Smiles's definitive *Lives of the Engineers*, admittedly written in 1862 before the major water-supply reservoirs were created, we are introduced to Rennie, Smeaton and Telford.[1] Angus Buchanan, the British industrial historian and biographer, in his *Engineers — A History of the Profession in Britain 1750–1914*, added Rankine, Bateman, Simpson and Hawksley — and this handful is only mentioned in passing.[2] L.T.C. Rolt, in his *Victorian Engineering*, additionally refers to George Deacon, who implemented Hawksley's designs for Liverpool's Lake Vyrnwy, and James Mansergh, who designed the Elan Valley dams.[3] Yet dam engineers surely must rank among the most important of professional engineers since, without adequate water supplies, public health and the welfare of nations are threatened to the point of unsustainability. Accordingly, this chapter will examine the biographies of these creative and determined individuals, drawing on the specialist works of Geoffrey Binnie and Donald Jackson.

Schoolchildren inspecting a beaver dam, c. 1899.

We might pause to reflect briefly on the reason for the apparent lack of prominence among dam engineers. Perhaps the reason is not too difficult to find. Dams have tended to be, at least since the nineteenth century, sited far from population centres — one thinks of the Elan Valley dams buried deep in the Cambrian Mountains and supplying the city of Birmingham more than 100 kilometres away, or the Hoover Dam in the remote Arizona desert. Dams were, of necessity, structures which were not in the public gaze (although admittedly some have become visitor attractions), unlike the bridges, tunnels, roads and railways used daily by the general public.

Dams were built in eighteenth-century Britain by landscape gardeners to create ornamental lakes for estate owners to enjoy. As we have seen, 'Capability' Brown thought nothing of moving a village to create a lake as a component of the view. Such dams were usually earth dams faced with puddle clay — clay thoroughly mixed with water and compacted with tampers. At Blenheim, Brown placed the clay as a central core, a technique initiated in Britain by John Grundy in Leicestershire in 1741 and at Grimsthorpe in 1748. This method, learned from the German experience of mining dams in the Harz Mountains in the sixteenth century, had been reported on by the Surveyor General John Taverner in 1600.[4] It became the trademark for the next generation of British dam engineers, particularly for reservoirs to feed canals. William Jessop and John Rennie were early exponents of dam-building for navigation with Rennie's specifications for a puddle-clay core the standard for more than a hundred years.

Arch spillways in ashlar masonry were perfected by John Smeaton for ironworks mills such as that for the Coquett Ironworks in Northumberland in 1776. This was an arched dam 50 metres wide with a radius of 52 metres. The curved wall had an outer skin of bonded and cramped masonry with a rubble core. As Smeaton said,

'There is not a more difficult or hazardous piece of work within the compass of civil enginery than the establishment of a high dam upon a rapid river.'[5] The dam on the Coquett still stands as testimony to the soundness of the design of this self-taught engineer.

Angus Buchanan termed these early pathfinders 'heroic engineers' since they had limited training and were largely self taught. Smeaton, the son of a solicitor, founded engineering (or 'engineery', as he called it) as a profession. Rejecting his parents' plans for him to follow in his father's footsteps, he was determined to pursue mechanics as a trade. He taught himself instrument-making and was elected as a Fellow of the Royal Society at the age of 29. In that same year he turned to engineering and with no previous experience was commissioned to design a water-mill in Lancashire. He went on to be responsible for bridges, river and canal navigations, mills, harbours and fen-drainage schemes.

In 1760 Smeaton met and became friends with John Grundy. Together they worked on the Louth Canal and the Witham Navigation. In 1771 Smeaton was instrumental in setting up the Society of Civil Engineers (known after his death as the Smeatonians). Most of the early members were associated with navigation or drainage schemes, but Grundy was the only one of the original eleven with any engineering training. The fact that they were almost all involved with such projects is not a coincidence: in this golden age of canals, Acts of Parliament were required and the engineers promoting them were called to London to give expert evidence. As a result, they would get together over dinner to discuss matters of mutual interest, and the Society was born. Smeaton coined the phrase 'civil engineer' (as distinct from the military Royal Engineers who received training at, among other locations, the Woolwich Royal Academy at Woolwich Barracks), but the Society was always seen as exclusive: 'gentleman engineer' would have been more accurate. On

Smeaton's death, Jessop, Rennie and others reorganized the Society (although it still only had 24 members) into three classes: Engineers, Gentlemen as honorary members, and Artists. The senior engineers were not keen to attract young engineers to their dining club. However, as Buchanan put it, 'they [the young engineers] found an ally . . . in . . . the person of Thomas Telford', who disliked the élite of the Society.[6] The Institution of Civil Engineers was formed in 1818 with Telford as its first President (which required a change of the rules restricting the age of members to 35).

By 1930 some 260 embankment dams more than 15 metres high had been built in the UK to Telford's design – mostly for water supply. The same technology was exported to the Empire, particularly India, where some 80 similar structures were built for water supply or irrigation.

Many of these dams were designed and supervised by a handful of engineers, including James Leslie, George Leather and his nephews John Towlerton Leather and John Wignall Leather, Thomas Hawksley, John F. La Trobe Bateman and Sir Robert Rawlinson. In the words of Schnitter, 'this resulted in a strong concentration of know-how and a remarkable degree of standardisation.' Schnitter suggested that this sound experience – rather than theory – explains why the British embankment dams were so safe and suffered only a handful of failures compared with the experience of the US, where 9 per cent of dams failed between 1850 and 1930.[7]

Buchanan extended this theory to what he perceived as 'dynasties' of engineers. Thus there were the Leathers, the Manserghs and especially the Binnies, starting with Alexander (later Sir Alexander) Binnie and continuing with his great grandson in the twenty-first century. The same applies to the family construction firms of Cubitt and McAlpine. There were also surrogate dynastic relationships when close and personal apprenticeships were served. Examples include John Smeaton's accommodation and pupillage of William Jessop, the son of his supervisor on the Eddystone Rock Lighthouse; William became resident engineer on the Aire and Calder Navigation for Smeaton, and later designed the East and West India Docks in London's Isle of Dogs.

We shall meet these names again in connection with the structures they designed, but mention must be made at this point of Edwin Chadwick, an Assistant on the Poor Law Commission of 1832. Chadwick became Secretary to the Poor Law Board in 1834, and the blame for much of the new system's severity was laid at his door.

Following an outbreak of typhus in 1838, Chadwick instigated an Inquiry that demonstrated the relationship between environment and health. This motivated him to investigate the living conditions of the poor – principally on the basis that funds could be saved if the poor could be kept from becoming a charge on the parishes in which they lived. The sanitary conditions of the labouring classes in Britain in 1842 revealed the true horrors of urban living at that time. The Health of Towns Commission was set up by the government under the chairmanship of the Duke of Buccleuch – the engineer Sir William Cubitt, who was to receive his knighthood in 1855 for his work on the Crystal Palace, was one of the Commissioners – with Chadwick as unofficial secretary. Evidence was given by a number of witnesses including Thomas Hawksley and Thomas Cubitt (no relation to William, he founded the contracting firm), who confirmed the inadequate condition of water supplies to major towns and cities.

The Inquiry led to many towns initiating water-supply schemes and to the engineers mentioned above supporting and designing schemes for Leeds, Nottingham, Sheffield, Liverpool and Manchester, as well as London. Chadwick, however, despaired of the piecemeal approach of these towns and formed the British, Colonial and

Foreign Drainage, Water Supply and Towns Improvement Company, which he persuaded Hawksley (then Engineer of the Trent Waterworks in Nottingham) to join as an engineer. This company gave Chadwick the opportunity to benefit from the works the Inquiry was recommending, and gave Hawksley the introduction to towns needing his services. Indeed Hawksley was soon to be approached by Boston (Lincolnshire), Lincoln and Coventry. His evidence to the Inquiry is often quoted:

> The most cleanly female . . . will invariably . . . relax her exertions under the influence of filth . . . and sink into a dirty, noisy, discontented and perhaps gin-drinking drab – the wife of a man who has no comfort in his house . . . The improvements certain to result from the introduction of water . . . into the houses of the working classes are far beyond the pecuniary advantages.[8]

Unfortunately for Chadwick, this was now also the time of railway mania with competition for funds, materials and labour, so commissions did not materialize as quickly and satisfactorily as he hoped. His company was wound up in 1849. Following accusations of self-serving interest, he resigned from the Board of Health in 1854 and never held public office again. However, in response to the identified need for a clean, reliable water supply, dam engineers prospered.

As we have seen, they were largely practical men who relied on their experience. That is not to deny that theory did not exist. As early as 1717, Henri Gautier of the French Corps of Bridge and Highway Engineers had published a treatise on the 'Slope of Repose' for earth retaining walls. Gautier recommended a mean thickness of 25 per cent of the height for an air-face inclination of 20 per cent – revised to 33 per cent by Bernard Forest de Bélidor in 1729. This became the standard reference for civil engineers in France,

Germany and Britain. A formula for calculating the stability of slopes in clay soils was proposed by the French military engineer Charles A. Coulomb in 1773, substantiated by the field observations of a slippage at Grosbois by Alexandre Collin, another member of the Corps. Unfortunately, despite these advances, French engineers were attracted to the emerging science of statics and consequently preferred masonry dams. Although Collin's concepts were to be revisited some 80 years later, the construction of embankment dams was effectively discontinued in France.

Other writers also had theories based on observation rather than rational mechanics. Don Pedro Bernardo Villarreal de Berriz, a Knight of the Order of Santiago and a Basque nobleman, owned mills in Vizcaya which were supplied with water by means of diversion dams. In 1736 he published *Maquinas Hydraulicas de Molinas y Herrerias*, in which he proposed the use of arch dams: 'when the river is narrow, one arch is sufficient and when it is wide, 2, 3, 4 or 5 will be needed.'[9] His dams still exist and are in use. He advocated a vertical water face and air faces sloping at 45 degrees for straight gravity dams and also gave meticulous instructions on construction including preparation and mortaring of joints.

As Norman Smith put it, up until 1850, while there had been a number of works written on dams, only Bélidor had adopted a rational scientific approach as opposed to empiricism. However, another member of the Corps of Bridge and Highway Engineers, J. Augustin Torterne de Sazilly, demonstrated a method of gravity-dam analysis showing that the most effective profile for such a dam is a triangle with a vertical upstream face. In his paper, published after his death in 1853, he visualized vertical slices through a dam and surmised that for the profile to be safe there should be equal compressive stress when the dam was empty as when it was full.

In 1858 Torterne de Sazilly's theories were put into practice when it was decided to protect Saint-Etienne in eastern France from flooding by the River Furens. The engineers were F.X.P. Emile Delocre and M. I. Auguste Graeff, again members of the Corps. The Furens Dam is 60 metres high and was built between 1859 and 1866 in a narrow gorge to a slight curve in plan. It is still in perfect condition – a monument to the engineers who made the first attempts to *design* dams. It revolutionized dam-building since it was so economical in terms of materials and labour.

Construction of earth embankment dams was still being carried out by means of pick and shovel at this time (with horsepower), but, in California in the 1860s, a Canadian, Anthony Chabot, used a technique borrowed again from the mining industry. Rather than excavating material by hand, a hydraulic method was employed. Earth and gravel were sluiced to the dam site by water jets and transferred by pipes, flumes or channels, then built up against the core of the dam. This technique reached its height in 1937 at Fort

'First dirt being pumped': Fort Peck Dam on the Missouri River, Montana. The largest hydraulically filled dam in the USA, completed in 1940.

Peck, which contains 95 million cubic metres of material – a quantity that would never have been economical to shift by hand.

Whatever the form of dam, it must be founded on competent rock foundations, and boreholes or trial pits are required to determine the depth of foundation needed. In the Harz Mountains in Germany, gunpowder was used in 1715 for the preparation of the Oder Dam, with the waste material having to be hauled out with shovel and barrow. The efficiency of the excavations for dams was improved by the invention of dynamite by the Swedish engineer Alfred Nobel in 1863 – and by the use of percussion drills to create holes for charges in the US from 1865. From the middle of the nineteenth century, work was made much quicker by the use of steam-powered shovels and narrow-gauge railways.

To avoid deep excavations, reinforcement of subsoil by the injection of cement was first tried in 1879 by Hawksley at Tunstall Dam

An Osgood steam-shovel building Morman Flat Dam, Arizona, in 1923.

(near Newcastle); the method was adopted by the US Bureau of Reclamation from 1915. (This technique, known as grouting, was to become standard throughout the world, reaching its zenith in 1990 at the 184-metre-high Ataturk Dam on the Euphrates in south-eastern Turkey. There, by means of 10 kilometres of tunnels and 1,200 kilometres of drill holes, 1,200,000 square metres of 'grout curtain' were placed to prevent leakage.)

Returning to the work of British engineers in India, the first masonry dam for water supply was completed in Pune in 1868. Henry Conybeare – who seems to have had a wide brief during his time in India, submitting designs for St John's Church in Bombay as well as

May 7, 1858.   THE BUILDING NEWS.   477

INLET TOWER, with a portion of the PRINCIPAL DAM of the VEHAR RESERVOIR of the BOMBAY WATERWORKS.
Engineer, Henry Conybeare, Esq., F.G.S., Mem. Inst. C.E.

The Vehar Dam built for Bombay Waterworks, 1858.

theory stood . . . on the same scientific basis, and of the same practical value, as the weather forecasts for the year in *Old Moore's Almanack*.'[11] Since Rankine had been dead for some nine years, he was no longer in a position to defend himself; engineers are more polite to one another these days. This is not the place to discuss the disparities and emphasis on theory and practice, but in Rankine's *Civil Engineering*, published in 1862, he referred to a method of creating a puddling-clay reservoir embankment: a flock of sheep was driven backwards and forwards along it several times! It was to be some 75 years before the Sheepsfoot Roller based on this 'principle' was developed.

After Rankine took the Chair at Glasgow in 1855, he eventually succeeded, in 1872, in establishing a degree in science. He published 111 papers prior to his early death, the last being on the design and construction of masonry dams in the *Engineer* (1872). Rankine developed a profile for a dam that almost completely eliminated tensile stress on horizontal sections, the first time this had been achieved by the application of scientific principles to dam design. His detailed *Report on the Design and Construction of Masonry Dams* (1872) explains the theories of stress in gravity dams and was put into effect at Periyar.

In 1877–8, a drought in Tamil Nadu led to widespread starvation, and many people died through lack of food and water. The Periyar scheme was revived by Pennycuick in 1882 for a concrete dam and received formal approval in 1887. The dam was to be made of concrete due to the absence of suitably skilled masons, and the concrete was faced with a thin skin of masonry. The project was formally inaugurated in September 1887 by Lord Connemara, Governor of Madras, by the felling of a tree: 'there could perhaps be no better symbolic function in a situation where the engineer is trying to find a way through dense uninhabited jungle.'[12]

And this was the problem. The dam site was kilometres from anywhere, in jungle inhabited by wild animals and where there would be a perpetual struggle with disease. Camps and quarters for the coolies and officers were laid out, together with first-aid posts. Initially there was no shortage of labour, but acclimatization took a long time, and 'many succumbed to malarial fever and the rest ran away as fast as they came in.'[13] The coolies were paid a day rate, but they always returned to their villages to attend to ploughing, sowing and harvesting. This, coupled with an eight-month working season to avoid the monsoon, meant that progress was slow. In 1889 and 1890 detachments of the First and Fourth Pioneer Corps were lent by the army for service on the construction, but the quality of their work was variable, and they were often withdrawn for military service so were not used again. However, a band of Portuguese carpenters arrived from Cochin – 'these were sober, quiet, religious men who were a pleasure to work with.'[14]

There were difficulties attracting and keeping masons, but, although their skills were often lacking, the quality of the materials more than compensated for this, and the dam remains in excellent condition (see illustration on p. 28). The dam site itself was 13 kilometres from the camp and depot at Thekkadi, and various options were considered for access over the Ghats. A canal with eleven locks was chosen, but this brought its own problems of working in isolated locations: 'the terror of wild beasts had to be faced.' Elephants were scared off with tom-toms and firebrands, and one man was killed by a tiger. Once tamed, the elephants were used for haulage. However, fever was the biggest problem: 'Deadly fever lurks behind the smiling countenance of Periyar.'[15] The combination of sun, rain and forest bred ideal conditions for malaria, but the coolies did not help themselves by their recklessness. Good food, warmth and filtered water would have helped, but they spent their wages on 'cheap jewellery, tinsel and "Manchester" goods'[16] (another example of British technology transfer). The importance of health and sanitation was recognized from the beginning.

Not all deaths were reported since the sick were often removed by relatives to either recover or die. Between 1892 and 1895 about 450 men died in the camps. It was to be expected perhaps that the camping of 5,000 people in a relatively small jungle area would lead to dubious sanitation conditions, and cholera epidemics occurred on two occasions. In a letter to the Chief Engineer, the Superintendent of Works reported on 11 March 1894: 'I have the honour to report that labour has fallen in consequence of the cholera to such a point that it is impossible to carry on work any longer.'[17] There were 45 fatalities in three weeks, and the camps were closed and moved to a new site. Despite disinfecting, burning and liming the ground, the cholera persisted, and when the number of men fell to 200 there was no alternative but to give up for the season.

Accidents were also common. The majority were associated with nitroglycerine or detonators – the labourers would remove the red flags indicating a misfire in the drill holes and claim payment, only to cause an explosion when their colleagues made a fresh charge. Deaths were so numerous that separate graveyards were earmarked for Indians and Europeans. As Pennycuick (now Col.) reported in 1893, he had anticipated that the work site would be declared a British Territory, but the Government of Madras did not agree; 'consequently the conditions of life . . . are by no means such as should prevail among a community of 6000 British subjects.' Twice construction works were washed away during the monsoon and the Madras Residency decided to abandon the project, but Pennycuick was determined to complete it. Allegedly, he returned to England and sold his property in order to raise the necessary funds to do so.

The dam (365 metres long plus a 'baby' dam of 73 metres and a 76-metre earth dam) was 54 metres tall (a world record for a concrete dam at the time) and constructed of a lime-*surki* concrete (lime, sand and *jaggary* – sugar pulp made from palm sap) faced with granite masonry set in a similar lime-*surki* mortar. The dam was completed in 1895 and inaugurated on 11 October by the Governor, Lord Wenlock. In 1931 the Maharani of Travangore built a lake palace for the Maharajah (Sree Chithira Tiuvnal) as a summer residence on a promontory in the resulting Periyar Lake – centred today on one of India's largest tiger reserves. Col. Pennycuick only guaranteed the dam for 50 years, and in 1990 it was reinforced by additional concrete on its air face and by cable-anchoring vertically through the masonry water face. A 2-kilometre tunnel through the Cardomom Hills to the other side of the water-shed to irrigate the fields of Tamil Nadu was integral to the project; in the 1960s the water was piped to a hydroelectric plant, adding to the usefulness of Kerala's Periyar Lake for the benefit of Tamil Nadu. This fact is not lost on the State of Kerala, in dispute as it is with Tamil Nadu, which wants to raise the dam's height.

The conditions at Periyar can be compared with those arranged for workers elsewhere – for example, on the contemporary Elan Valley scheme for Birmingham, which was started in 1892. The Birmingham Waterworks Company was granted parliamentary powers to supply water in 1826. The company's first engineer was John Rofe, who was succeeded by his son Henry in 1829 (the consulting engineers Rofe, Kennard and Lapworth were later responsible for many British reservoir schemes between the 1960s and the 1990s). In the course of representations for the adoption of the Public Health Act of 1849, the government-appointed inspector, Robert Rawlinson, reported that the town's water supply was unsatisfactory, and the company extended the area of constant supply in 1853.

The Mayor of Birmingham, Joseph Chamberlain, obtained powers to acquire the Waterworks Company in the interests of public health in accordance with the Birmingham Corporation Water Act, 1875. During the period preceding the acquisition, the Corporation had concluded that it would be necessary to look elsewhere for supplies large enough to meet the needs of the rapidly growing city. In 1870 attention was drawn to the mid-Wales mountains as a potential source, and, in 1871, Rawlinson was instructed 'to inquire as to the Water Supply of Birmingham compared to other Towns . . . and to avail [himself] of the services of [consulting engineers] Lawson and Mansergh to make such surveys as required'.[18]

James Mansergh had been apprenticed to Lawsons, engineers of Lancaster, at the age of fifteen. At 21 he had gone to Brazil and worked on the Rio de Janeiro railway. He returned to England in 1859 and worked for a while on the railways of mid-Wales before entering into partnership with his brother-in-law John Lawson in Westminster. During his career he gave evidence at some 300 public inquiries and made more than 600 appearances in both Houses of Parliament.

Rawlinson examined the existing water quality and yields from boreholes, streams and potential new sources from rivers around Birmingham. He concluded that nearby sources were all too polluted or in catchments which were agricultural and heavily manured, and therefore likely to be of unsuitable quality in the future. His criteria for site selection, and his recommendations, were that ideally the water provided should be capable of delivery to storage areas in Birmingham under gravity and that, in order to provide for future expansion of the city, an area of watershed on uncultivated land in excess of current requirements should be selected – criteria which could well apply today.

Rawlinson looked at five river catchments in mid-Wales and con-cluded that the Elan and Claerwen were 'much superior and in fact nothing better can be found in the country nor could better be desired', being 'almost utterly devoid of human habitation . . . and other sources of pollution . . . [and] . . . almost totally uncultivated'. Although his estimates for development of the various catchments identified the Elan and Claerwen as the most expensive, he recom-mended their utilization for the purity of supply in an area unlikely to be developed – i.e. a 'remote corner of Radnorshire far away from any large town or great line of traffic [thus ensuring] its remaining in its present condition for many years'. He described the area as 'a solitude, tenanted only by a few straggling flocks of sheep'.[19]

The Corporation was unable to promote and secure a new sup-ply source until it had acquired the Waterworks Company. Local extensions to the supply system proved satisfactory until 1890, when Mansergh was consulted (Rawlinson was 80 and retired by this time); he still recommended the Elan and Claerwen scheme. In his Proof of Evidence in support of the Bill to the House of Lords Committee in 1892, he set out the grounds for his preference, describing the area's population, the catchment, water sources and future requirements. Again he looked at alternative sources but concluded that they 'all ran through highly-manured agricultural country, with towns, villages and farms and are inevitably pol-luted'. The area he recommended was very sparsely populated, 'and the extent of cultivated land is exceedingly small'. Clearly the requirement for good-quality water directed the engineers towards catchments where there was little cultivation: 'it is a good source of supply (I should have been a noodle to suggest any but the best I knew of).'[20] A Water Bill (to secure the finances for the scheme) was authorized by a poll of burgesses of the city on 9 December 1891.

For a description of the area in which the dams were to be built, the most useful source is Eustace Tickell, who, before work could begin, was sent by Mansergh along with Mansergh's two sons to carry out the surveying. Tickell later became the engineer in charge of Pen-y-Gareg (Above the Stone) Dam and made pen-and-ink sketches of the river valleys prior to inundation. He compiled these, together with his own commentary and contributions by Mansergh and William Rossetti (Shelley's biographer), into a commemorative volume that was presented by the 'Water Committee to those landowners who co-operated with Birmingham in allowing the pipeline to be carried through their estates'.[21] After completing work on the dams, Tickell went to Ceylon to build railways.

Two houses in the valleys that were destroyed by the reservoirs had 'some pretensions and literary interest, namely Cwm Elan on the bank of the Elan . . . and Nantgwillt on the bank of the Claerwen . . . Both of these houses . . . were associated with the poet Shelley'.[22] Shelley had originally arrived at Cwm Elan, a remote house at the top of the valley, on 9 July 1811, and had written to his friend Thomas Jefferson Hogg that the scenery was 'divine, but all very stale flat and unprofitable – indeed this place is a very great bore'.[23] He clearly suffered a mood swing the next day when he wrote to Elizabeth Hitchener, 'rocks [are] piled on to each other to tremendous heights, rivers formed into cataracts by their projections, and valleys clothed with woods, present an appearance of enchantment'.[24] In April of the following year, on his return from Ireland with his first wife Harriet, Shelley negotiated for the lease of Nantgwillt but only stayed for two months.

Given this association, Tickell focused his sketches on these valleys and houses, and in his preface to the plates he described the locality as

one of the most charming valleys in Great Britain, scenes which are soon
to be lost for ever . . . And the valleys where now the river flows through
moor and bracken, woodland and meadow, will in a few years be converted into a chain of lakes. Beautiful lakes they will doubtless be, wind-
ing up the valleys with sinuous margins, wooded promontories such as
are seen on Derwentwater, frowning crags and screes which will remind
one of Wastwater. But their construction dooms many a picturesque and
interesting spot to destruction and it would be indeed a pity if they
should be allowed to pass away without some record.[25]

Tickell's words provide an insight into the perception of the valleys by an engineer at the time. He recorded the future loss of
Nantgwillt and Cwm Elan together with the chapels, schoolhouse
and about twenty farmsteads:

But in reviewing this roll call it must be remembered that, *sad as it is*
[emphasis added] it would be more difficult to find in this island a place

Cwm Elan, Powys, where Percy Bysshe Shelley briefly stayed, sketched by Eustace Tickell,
resident Engineer on the Elan Valley scheme, in 1894.

where more than 70 square miles of land could be taken for a public purpose without dispossessing very many more people and destroying many more houses. At the same time, the seclusion of the valley is one of its greatest charms. It lies hidden away amongst the mountains and leads to nowhere. The valley is visited by few . . . but those who have known it will never forget the charm of the scenery . . . [26]

Mansergh described the proposed 'Birmingham Water Scheme' in the following terms:

The determination of the area of watershed to be acquired was a comparatively easy problem [considered from a water engineer's point of view] because the contraction of the valley at Caban Coch and the opening out above of the wide expanse of flat land fixed at once the position of the dam of the lowest reservoir.

While recognizing that

the mansion and beautiful grounds of Nantgwillt [will] be drowned . . . when more than full, the water will overflow from all the reservoirs in picturesque cascades down the faces of the dams . . . [in maximum flood] forming probably the finest waterfall in this country.[27]

Mansergh as the designer therefore was aware both of the loss of features and of what would be put in their place.

The Birmingham Corporation Water Bill met with opposition in Birmingham itself, along the route of the aqueduct and in areas affected by the construction of the reservoirs. Provision for supply to adjacent counties within 15 miles of the aqueduct had already been agreed – this arrangement became known as the Birmingham Conditions. However, Welsh MPs objected to the Bill on the grounds of the effects on Wales and the River Wye. Mr Shaw-Lefevre MP, 'champion of the Preservation of the Commons' and founder of the Commons and Open Spaces Preservation Society in 1865, proposed access to the hills and common rights on the watershed. At the second reading of the Bill, the Corporation accepted his conditions.

The Corporation sensibly reached an agreement with Mr Lewis Lloyd, the principal landowner in the watershed, and the withdrawal of opposition from landowners greatly accelerated the passage of the Bill through Committee. It was finally approved, receiving Royal Assent on 27 June 1892. It would appear that landowner opposition fell away once compensation was agreed; as Thomas Barclay put it, 'the local opposition . . . was of a very feeble character.'[28]

In his evidence to Parliament, Mansergh had stated that 'all dams shall be built of masonry because there are sound rock foundations for all of them . . . and because material for earthen dams with puddle cores is not procurable in the district.' Mansergh died in 1905, and it was left rather belatedly to his sons to present a paper to the ICE in 1912 in which they described the design and construction of the dams. 'The first three dams were all to be of a greater height than any previously in this country and cross section demanded careful consideration. In 1895 the Bouzey dam near Epinard in France gave way and margins of safety were built into the design.'[29] The dams serving Birmingham were built of cyclopean rubble, faced with block-in-course masonry. The rubble 'plums' — up to 10 tons in weight — were set in Portland-cement concrete. This technique was an innovation at the time, replacing the use of dressed blocks bedded in mortar. The valve tower, part of the masonry structure of the dam, was described as being 'surmounted by a handsome octagonal valve house with a domed roof.'[30] The Foel Valve Tower is circular with a domed roof covered with copper and marks the entrance to the 117-kilometre aqueduct to Frankley Service Reservoir in Birmingham.

In addition to these works, the Corporation built a temporary railway and permanent highway, a church, a Baptist chapel and a school to take the place of those submerged in Caban Coch. Alexander Binnie remarked that when he and James Mansergh had been working on the mid-Wales railway in 1862–3, they had imagined dams on the spot where they were eventually built. Walter Hunter (a Director of the Grand Junction Company), purporting to represent 'the mouth of an artist', noted that

the appearance of ugliness was due to critics not understanding that adaptability had beauty of its own and that it was rather lack of education which caused a man not to appreciate engineering works even though outwardly they might not seem to be as beautiful as some other works. The works of engineers could be carried out to harmonize with

The Pen-y-Gareg Dam in the Elan Valley, nearing completion in 1905.

their situations, and the reservoirs of the Birmingham works had added to the beauty of the scenery.[31]

The scheme was opened in July 1904 when King Edward VII opened the valves at Foel Tower.

The overall engineer in charge had been George Yourdi, son of an Irish mother and a Greek father. Yourdi had been in charge of the labour force, which at times numbered as many as 1,500 navvies ('navigators') and engineers. He was a strict disciplinarian; an engineer who went for a few beers in the local town of Rhayader was dismissed on his return since 'someone in his position should not frequent public houses.'[32] Unusually for the time, Yourdi had degrees in arts and engineering and was a Fellow of Trinity College Dublin. For eight years this single man never spent a night out of the valley. He lived in Nantgwillt House — previously occupied by Shelley and his wife Harriet — which is alleged to have inspired Francis Brett Young to write 'The House under the Water'.

The opening of the Elan Valley scheme by Edward VII and Queen Alexandra, 21 July 1904. A special train ran from Rhayader station along the tracks laid for construction.

The work force was comparatively well looked after: a complete 'model' village was built, comprising huts for the the workers and public buildings including a school, hospital, mission room, canteen, police station, fire station with engines and post office. There was a full range of services, including sewerage, water supply, lighting and fire hydrants (all buildings were constructed of wood). The huts came in four classes, ranging from those for ordinary lodgers (for up to eight men, a hut keeper and his wife) to those for officials and married men. Visitors from Rhayader were amazed to see that the navvies 'slept in beds. With sheets. Like *people*'.[33] In 1897, Queen Victoria's Jubilee Day was a paid holiday and the whole village descended on Rhayader, where they consumed the victuals for the day provided by the Jubilee Committee in less than an hour.

Many of the navvies were Irish (two-thirds working on the Cray Dam for Swansea in 1900 were Irish), and at Elan, unusually, one was black – he is recorded as having died of exposure in the hills above Rhayader in 1897. Another death was of Thomas Pugh, who accidentally shot himself with a pistol he was repairing in the blacksmith's shop in 1898. The canteen was only open for five hours a day, and customers were limited to six pints (Allsopps Single X or bottled Bass) and no women, singing, juggling or marbles. The village was strictly policed, and access was only possible via a single suspension bridge with a bridge janitor. (Although it was reported that the men built a small footbridge across the Elan so that, having been thrown out of the canteen, they could cross down to Rhayader to get truly drunk and then spend the night in the hedgerows – this was fine during the summer, but many died from hypothermia during the winter).[34]

How many men died in the construction of the first phase of the Elan Valley dams is not recorded, but Yourdi's records show his expenses for telegrams to next of kin for 1902, during which three men died, including John Jones in January (falling from a gantry at Caban Dam) and Samuel Davies in December (as a result of an explosion in the quarry). In 1903 Yourdi paid a total of £9 10s to Evan Jones for the loss of ten sheep killed by the supply train. That same year, there was a smallpox outbreak – five cases were reported, one of which was fatal.

Of the proposed six dams only three were built, with the intention of adding the others as the need arose. In the event, it was decided that one additional dam would suffice. This received approval in 1939 but, due to the war, was not begun until 1950, when Birmingham Corporation invited tenders for the new Claerwen Dam. Various options were proposed, but the Corporation opted for a masonry-clad curved gravity dam 'to match the appearance of those existing'.[35] (There was a shortage of skilled masons in Britain at this time; they had to be brought from Italy to work on the dam.)

At the end of the nineteenth century, British expertise moved from its proving ground in India to another country in need of agricultural advancement – Egypt. As Norman Smith put it, '[This is] a particularly interesting case of technology transfer in the sense that expertise passed from one country to another without ever having been an activity indigenous to the native land of its engineers.'[36]

In 1883 Colin Scott-Moncrieff, who had been an irrigation engineer in British India, arrived to take charge of Egypt's Irrigation Department and Works. He brought with him William Willcocks, who, at the age of 31, had never set foot outside of India; as Willcocks himself put it, he had been born 'in a tent on the bank of an irrigation canal in India'.[37] After engineering college, he had spent ten years on drainage works on the Ganges and the construction of the Paricha weir on the Betwa Canal. In 1890 he began his study of Egypt's irrigation under the title of Director General of Reservoir Studies. In three years he surveyed the 1,200 kilometres of the Nile and its desert margins – an extraordinary achievement in such a short time. During the final season he dispensed with the luxury of a tent. Every morning he is alleged to have memorized lines from Bunyan or the Bible (eventually committing the whole of the New Testament to memory). A colonial misfit in the narrow social world of the expatriate British, Willcocks had no time for dinners and dances and probably related more to the farmers along the Nile than to his supervisors. It was said that 'every fellah in Egypt knows the name of Wilguks.'[38] As Scott-Moncrieff said, 'he is not the conventional type of man.' Willcocks selected a site at Aswan for a dam and an 'International Commission' was appointed to assess his choice. The commission comprised Sir Benjamin Baker, President-elect of the ICE, Auguste Boulé of France and Giacomo Torricelli of Italy. Although they agreed on the choice of dam site, the three are reported to have had different reactions to their assignment. Boulé liked good food, Baker ate anything, while Torricelli's staple diet was Chianti and macaroni. Willcocks lived on apricots, rice and whisky.[39]

The dam as proposed was 1,950 metres long with 180 sluices which could be opened in sequences to allow the silt-laden floods to pass through for irrigation and then to hold back seasonal flows in the reservoir for later release. Storage was an issue, however, and environmental concerns played an important role even in 1895: the proposed storage of 2.5 cubic kilometres was reduced to 1 cubic kilometre to prevent the flooding of the Temple of Isis. Winston Churchill pronounced that 'the State must struggle and the people starve in order that professors may exult and tourists find some space on which to scratch their names.'[40] Willcocks's original design was influenced by the Betwa Dam with its 'long sweeping curves'. However, the Commission decided on a straight alignment. Willcocks disagreed, believing that an arch dam would

SCIENTIFIC AMERICAN

[Entered at the Post Office of New York, N. Y., as Second Class Matter. Copyright, 1901, by Munn & Co.]

A WEEKLY JOURNAL OF PRACTICAL INFORMATION, ART, SCIENCE, MECHANICS, CHEMISTRY, AND MANUFACTURES.

Vol. LXXXIV.—No. 18.
[Established 1845.]

NEW YORK, MAY 4, 1901.

[$3.00 A YEAR.
5 CENTS A COPY.

Nile Reservoir Works, Assiut—Upstream Side of Piers, Looking West.

Assouan Dam—Water Rushing Through Central Sluices.

Work at the West Bank, Assiut.

Centrifugal Pumps at the Foundation Excavations.

Composite Metal and Masonry Construction, Assouan.

CONSTRUCTION OF THE GREAT NILE RESERVOIR.—[See page 279.]

First Aswan Dam under construction, 1901.

be stronger in the event that its height would have to be raised — which eventually happened twice!

As at the Elan Valley, a factor in the Aswan design was the recent collapse of the Bouzey Dam. Baker — now the dam's engineer — drew the conclusion that the recent theories of gravity-dam design were not at fault but that they had been disregarded at Bouzey. However, the Aswan design was complicated by the need for so many sluices.

The workforce in this desert location approached 15,000 on occasion, comprising mostly native workers and a contingent of skilled labour from Britain and stone-cutters from Italy. The camp built for them was impressive: this 'European' village included shops, a restaurant and a hospital. An ice-making machine was provided, principally for the hospital. Neither was it all work and no play with cricket, football and tennis pursued enthusiastically. On Christmas Day 1901 a football match was held between the Scottish and English members of staff. Sir Murdoch MacDonald was centre forward and the game ended in a 1—1 draw despite three members of the Scottish team having to be carried from the field in the first quarter of an hour when the after effects of the Christmas festivities proved too much. In contrast to Periyar, no serious epidemic occurred; the hospital was principally kept busy attending to cases of sunstroke and accidents with explosives.

An added bonus of the first Aswan Dam was that it provided a series of locks to negotiate the Aswan Cataract. Although he was knighted for his contributions, Willcocks left the project in 1897 when his relationship with MacDonald, the new Resident Engineer, deteriorated. The finishing stone was laid on 10 December 1902 by Princess Marguerite Louise of Prussia, but already there were plans to raise the dam to its original proposed height (and flood the Temple of Isis). Baker now had the task of raising the dam and, at the same time, ensuring the free flow and operation of all 180 sluices.

A further complication was the publication in 1904 of a paper by Pearson and Atcherley entitled 'On Some Disregarded Points in the Stability of Masonry Dams' and proposing that previous calculations based only on horizontal stresses did not tell the full story since they ignored vertical ones. This alarmist paper was based on tests on strips of wood and was not really applicable to dams. However, it gave rise to a controversy that lasted for four years with full exposure in the engineering journals. Factions were formed favouring the 'mathematician's dam' and the 'engineer's dam', and the controversy was eventually resolved by India-rubber models constructed by J. S. Wilson – an assistant to Baker at Aswan – and William Gore, who had assisted George Deacon at Vyrnwy. The models proved that the prevailing methods of designing dams were sound and also pioneered the tradition of dam design by the use of models which prevailed throughout the twentieth century.

Baker, who died in 1907, realized that fixing a 'new' dam to the old one at Aswan would cause problems due to differentials in temperature in the desert; a space for expansion was therefore initially left between the two structures. On 23 December 1912 many of the attendees at the first opening of the Aswan Dam were called back to witness the second inauguration ten years and two weeks after the first.

By 1918 Murdoch MacDonald had established that both Egypt and the Sudan could be irrigated by management of the Nile. However, Willcocks, whom MacDonald had replaced as Director General of Reservoirs, did not agree and became increasingly virulent in his opposition, accusing MacDonald of falsifying the flow records. He turned a 'serious situation into a disastrous one with the publication in Cairo of *The Nile Projects*.'[41] This document stretched to 200 pages of criticism of the honesty and competence of Willcocks's fellow professionals. It is without equal in the history of engineering both in its vitriolic attacks and in its effect on its author.

Willcocks's obsession with MacDonald's figures ended with his being found guilty of criminal slander and libel in the Consular Court in Cairo in 1921. It has been said that at this point 'an illustrious career came to a tragic end',[42] but Willcocks returned to India, where in a report published in 1930, two years before his death, he explained the irrigation-canal system of the Ganges — which previous British engineers had thought were for navigation. (The British police, mistakenly but forcefully, tried to stop the peasants breaking the canal banks at night to fertilize and irrigate their fields). Willcocks proposed the restoration of these ancient works to 'bring in again the health and wealth which . . . Bengal once enjoyed'.[43] On his death, the *Spectator* wrote that the Aswan Dam was 'as great a memorial as Cheops' Pyramid, and of considerably more use to Egyptians'.

The single most important milestone in embankment-dam theory was the publication in 1926 of 'Principles of Soil Mechanics' by Karl von Terzaghi. Terzaghi was to dominate approaches to the stability of earth dams from then on. By 1940 the elements of earth-dam theory were established, enabling the construction of higher and bigger earth dams. This process was also encouraged by improved methods of construction.

From the 1930s on, earth-moving machinery replaced horsepower. Embankment dams were particularly amenable to the mechanization of construction, and changes accelerated in the 1930s and '40s due to advances in construction equipment. Bulldozers were attached to caterpillar tractors and used for excavation work as well as for the spreading of material. Advances in both power and tyres meant that vehicles could work on embankments as well

as excavation sites and on haul roads. Sheepsfoot rollers were used for compaction from 1905 and had become standard by the 1930s.

Dam-building in the US in the 1900s was largely the result of home-grown talent – again mostly self taught. However, while the British sphere of influence did not extend beyond the Empire, later émigrés from Europe did add to the rich variety of dam structures produced.

The innovative and self-taught model is epitomized by the career of John S. Eastwood. Eastwood was motivated by one principal interest – economy – but this led to two other attributes of what David Billington described as 'Structural Art': efficiency and elegance.[44] Eastwood created more than 60 dams in his career but was frequently faced with opposition from conservative-minded engineers who sought to stir up public concern at his 'airy arches'.[45]

Horse teams were still used, especially for embankment dams, in the early part of the twentieth century.

Eastwood had been born in Minnesota in 1857 and on leaving college had gone out to the Pacific Northwest, building railways. Eventually in 1883 he settled in Fresno, California, and explored the Sierra Nevada. He became involved in the logging of the Giant Sequoia, which – in contrast to John Muir, who saw beauty – he saw as a resource to be utilized.

The 1887 Wright Act had authorized the creation of Irrigation Districts through bond sales. Eastwood succeeded Hermann Schussler as engineer to the Sunsea Irrigation District south of Fresno. In the 1890s he became one of the pioneers in hydroelectricity, which was to transform California's culture and economy; he formed the San Joaquin Electric Company in 1895. This failed when the competing Fresno Gas and Electric Company diverted water away from Eastwood's sources – at the time of one of California's severest droughts. The lesson was learned: adequate water storage was mandatory. In 1901 Eastwood proposed a dam on the San Joaquin River to enlarge several lakes in the catchment in order to supply the Mammoth Power Company, which sold electricity to San Francisco. This scheme never materialized, but in 1902 he became involved in the much larger Big Creek power scheme, for which he proposed an arch-buttressed concrete dam – what he later described as a multiple-arch dam. The design was based on an aspiration to save on concrete, and in this Eastwood succeeded.

An earth-fill dam would have used 49,000 cubic metres of concrete (and 1,025,000 cubic metres of earth), a gravity dam 245,000 cubic metres, but Eastwood's proposal only envisaged 59,000 cubic metres of concrete. The scheme was delayed since it was in the Federally owned Sierra National Park, and President Theodore Roosevelt sought protection of this natural resource. While he waited for the consent to be negotiated, Eastwood built a dam of similar

design for the Hume-Bennett Lumber Company. This was 200 metres long and 20 metres tall and had twelve arches. Remarkably, it was built in 114 working days. On the basis of Hume Lake he accepted a commission to build a replacement for Frank E. Brown's Bear Valley Dam in San Bernadino. James D. Schuyler had proposed a rock-fill dam at an estimated $140,000, but Eastwood's design was costed at $80,000. It was to be 110 metres long and 24 metres tall with ten arches and with strut tie-beams through the buttresses.

Rather than timber formwork for the arches, Eastwood used corrugated steel, which was left in place and covered with a cement plaster. Big Bear made his name as a dam engineer – he was now associated with one of the world's most famous thin-arch dams. As he himself put it, he had seen Brown's dam as 'a long step in the right direction' and his own contribution as 'further strides towards the Ultimate Dam'.[46] In the event, Big Creek was built by Stone and Webster to a curved-mass gravity design, but this rebuff did not concern Eastwood – he had arrived. Big Bear withstood overtopping by floods in 1916 and an earthquake in 1918, which

'The Ultimate Dam'. John S. Eastwood's ten-arch concrete dam, which replaced (and submerged) the Bear Valley Dam, California, in 1901.

went a long way to raise the confidence of Eastwood's clients in the 1920s. In 1924 a road was built over the dam.

In 1911 Eastwood prepared a design for Big Meadows Dam upstream from Sacramento for the Great Western Power Company (GWPC). Despite positive reviews from Schuyler and Alfred Noble, the GWPC also sought the opinion of the East Coast hydraulic engineer John R. Freeman. Freeman was much in favour of gravity dams:

> it does not pay to carry economy to excess in dam building and there is nothing quite so satisfying as a big solid mass of concrete – Eastwood's airy arches and lace curtain effect [are] not well suited to inspire public confidence; [he] has become so impressed with multiple arch designs that I presume he will ultimately have his hair trimmed in scallops.[47]

Eastwood responded that 'the solid dam would soon be placed with other relics of the dark ages where it belongs – in the junk heap.'[48] Nevertheless, Freeman succeeded in persuading the GWPC that the arch dam was unsound, and – with half of it built – it was abandoned.

Eastwood was never to be involved in hydroelectric schemes again and promoted himself purely as a dam builder – 'the Eastwood Multiple Arch Dam – the Last Word in Dams'. He moved to Oakland in 1911, and at the 1914 Internal Waterways Congress in San Francisco he pronounced (echoing Churchill) 'the Californian slogan e're should be, that 'tis a crime to let our rivers reach the sea.' He had to search for work at this time but, following the successful construction of the Mountain Dell Dam for Salt Lake City in 1917, gained a number of commissions from the Mormon community, including his longest multiple-arch dam – the 792-metre Fish Creek Dam in Carey, Idaho (1919).

Eastwood always sought to refine and improve his designs and in 1921 conceived the curved-face concept for the Cave Creek Dam in Phoenix, Arizona. Cave Creek was usually dry but in rainstorms became a torrent, and the dam was needed to protect Phoenix from floods. It was 515 metres long and 36 metres high with 38 arches, which were only 0.5 metres thick at the top and 1 metre at the bottom – thus having a curved profile and saving even more concrete. Construction started in March 1922, and, despite being held up (ironically) for lack of water for the mixing of concrete, it was completed in February of the following year. Almost immediately it stopped a flood, and, as the *Arizona Gazette*[49] reported, 'already more than paid for itself'. Concrete was carried from a central mixing plant in a Ford truck, and then the hopper was lifted from the truck by a Brown hoist crane and the concrete placed in the formwork.

More dams followed, including the Anyox Dam in British Columbia, which was Canada's tallest dam for many years and of which it was said that 'it's a pity [that such a pleasing design] is in such a remote place.'[50] Eastwood's last project – still searching for that 'Ultimate Dam' – was a 'triple-arch' dam at Webber Creek near Placesville in Northern California. His design was still founded on economy since, although his dams were cheaper than other forms, unit costs were higher, so he sought more efficient construction techniques. This had just one large centre arch of 43 metres with smaller arches of 33 metres on either side. It was 27 metres high and was impounding water in March 1924 when Eastwood inspected it a few months before he died.

His most ambitious project – like so many – was never built: a 915-metre-long, 92-metre-tall dam at Balojaque in Mexico. His plans for a triple-arch dam 122 metres tall on the Colorado River would have flooded the Grand Canyon. His obituary in the *Southwest Builder and Contractor* recorded 'always the seer, the prophet of things to be, the

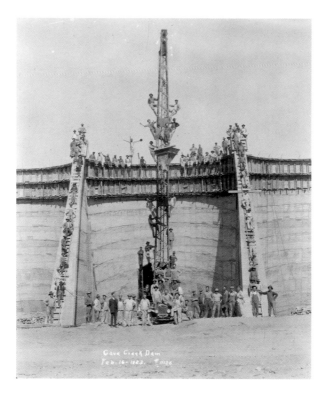

dreamer who saw far into the future, and who happily for us, was able to make some of his dreams come true'.[51]

Back in the UK, earth dams were still largely the order of the day, but one stands out for a number of reasons. The 457-metre-long Silent Valley Dam was built between 1923 and 1932 in the Mourne Mountains to supply Belfast. The Belfast City and District Water commissioners had recognized the need for increasing water storage to meet the requirements of the growing industrial city in the 1890s and had purchased the whole of the 3,600-hectare catchment by 1899. They then took the extraordinary step of building a 35-kilometre-long wall round the catchment! This was started in 1904 and was a double-thickness rough granite structure 1.75 metres in height. It was known as the Back Ditch to the men who built it —

Eastwood's concrete dam at Cave Creek, Phoenix, under construction in 1922.

they worked from March to October, camping out overnight in the summer months. It was finally completed in 1922, and the contract for the dam was signed in March 1923 – a year after Ulster's partition. Designed and supervised by Fred W. McCullough (until his sudden death in 1927, when William Binnie, Edward Sandeman and H. Prescot Hill took over), this dam was notable in that the contractor's engineers team included Dorothy Buchanan, the first woman to become a corporate member of the ICE. Gangs of labourers were hired by the contractors to walk back and forth over the clay core to heel it in. They wore special boots with steel tips and heels which had to be 'Vaselined' every night to stop the clay from sticking to them. Belfast men apparently didn't like the puddling:

> They're working in the puddle clay
> They're working night and day
> The men who come from Belfast
> We know they will not stay[52]

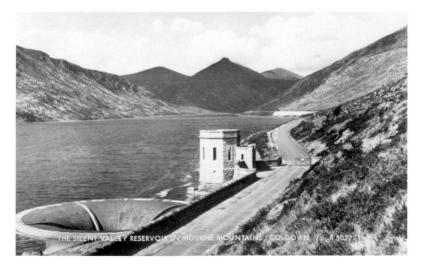

THE SILENT VALLEY RESERVOIR IN MOURNE MOUNTAINS, CO. DOWN   R 5027

The Silent Valley reservoir, Co. Down, for Belfast, completed in 1928. In 1951 a two-and-a-half mile brick-lined tunnel was dug (by candlelight) to transfer water from the adjacent Annalong catchment to Silent Valley.

While men were still employed for the puddling of clay, mechanization was gradually entering the field of dam-building in Europe as in the US. Dan Dooley, who had joined the Silent Valley project from the irrigation scheme on the Blue Nile, was a master operator of his Ruston steam excavator and filled 500 trucks in a day (including breaks for bacon and eggs fried on a shovel in the firebox), for which achievement he received a watch and a £15 bonus at a time when skilled wages were only £2 a week. (C. S. Lewis's Narnia in *The Lion, the Witch and the Wardrobe* comprised the Mournes and the Silent Valley: 'I feel that at any moment a giant might raise his head over the next ridge.' The men who built that wall *were* giants indeed.) For the placing of stonework, however, there was never going to be a substitute for labour.

Concrete was first used in dam-building in the 1870s in the US and Switzerland but was still mixed by hand. Mechanical mixing was used at the Abbeystead Dam for the water supply of Lancaster in 1881, and in 1890, at Crystal Springs, San Francisco, Hermann Schussler devised a method of mixing in drums turned by steam power and then transporting the concrete in hand-carts on rails to the dam site, where it was formed into interlocking blocks. It was spread in thin layers and rammed manually. The engineers realized that the cement content of the concrete had to be limited due to the heat it developed during curing. Consequently, contraction joints were provided (which were later filled); these also acted as cooling slots.

The use of water circulated through pipes in the concrete was first introduced at the Merwin arch dam in Washington State in 1931, and later ice was used instead in the concrete mix. At the Presa de Rules Dam in southern Spain, completed in 2002, the daytime temperatures reached 42 °C and cooling pipes (nicknamed 'pythons')

were incorporated within the concrete. (From the mid-1950s, fly ash from power stations was used in the concrete mix to reduce the cement content and the heat generated.) Compacting of the concrete was achieved at the Morris Dam east of Los Angeles in 1932 by the use of immersed vibrators. All of these technical developments were embodied in the Hoover Dam.

Even though dam projects became larger, they were naturally only as good as the designers or the engineers driving them. The Hoover Dam on the Nevada–Arizona border was designed by John L. Savage of the Bureau of Reclamation before being put out to tender in 1931. (Savage went on to help on the Three Gorges dam in the 1940s.) It was such a major task that it would use as much concrete as all of the projects in the Bureau's previous 29 years put

Placing stonework by hand on the 54 m high Marathon Dam in 1928 for the water supply of Athens. The stone is pentelikon marble as used for the Parthenon.

together. The Six Companies consortium (comprising some now household names such as Bechtel and Kaiser) brought in Frank T. Crowe as General Superintendent, first to prepare the bid (he came in at $48,890,996 — just $24,000 more than the Bureau's engineer's estimate) and then, having won it, to see it built.

Men like Crowe were more than resident engineers. 'I was wild to build that dam — it was the biggest dam ever built by anyone, anywhere', he said in a 1943 interview. Born in 1882 in Quebec, he was a student at the University of Maine when a guest speaker from the newly formed Reclamation Service inspired him to sign on for a summer job — he stayed for twenty years. Having become the Bureau's General Superintendent of Construction – and having devised efficient methods of construction such as cableways for concrete distribution — he left to join Morrison-Knudsen to do what he liked best: build dams. A driven man, Crowe had already supervized dams in Wyoming, California and Idaho when the big one came along. He features in Bruce Murkoff's novel *Waterborne*.[53] He

The reaction of cement with water causes heat to be liberated. At Grand Coulee Dam, Washington State, cold water was circulated through miles of pipe embedded in the dam. During excavation a mud slide was halted by freezing it with secondhand ice-making machinery.

also took the men (made infamous by John Steinbeck) who were fleeing west in 1931 in search of work and fortune – Murkoff's 'dam bums', skilled men who only knew dams – and turned them into builders of one of the era's greatest industrial monuments.

When Crowe arrived in Las Vegas on 11 March 1931, at the age of 49, a week after the bids had been opened, he set about building Boulder City. He completed (Boulder) Hoover Dam two years ahead of schedule in February 1936 but not without a few short cuts. He allowed ordinary motor vehicles to be used in the construction of the diversion tunnels, and many men were gassed by the carbon monoxide. The State of Nevada took Six Companies to court where Crowe swore that no one had been gassed working underground – eventually the company settled out of court.

Hoover Dam introduced a number of innovations. Men were taken to the work site each day from Boulder City in 150-seat wagons. Once on site, they were carried across the canyon on cables – as was the concrete from the batching plant. However, the dangerous job of removing loose rock and making 'keys' for the abutments had to be carried out by hand. For this, men called 'high scalers' swung and abseiled themselves down the face of the canyon.

After Hoover Dam, Crowe worked on Parker Dam, Copper Basin and Gene Wash dams on the Colorado, and the kilometre-long, curved gravity Shasta Dam in Northern California. He retired in 1944 and died two years later.

By the time the Grand Coulee Dam was started by Roosevelt in 1934 in Washington State, contractors were accomplished in their organization of such multi-million-dollar schemes. Grand Coulee was not as high as Hoover but was to be three and a half times longer and would use as much concrete as it would have taken to build three ancient Egyptian pyramids. In *The Dam* by H. M. Newell, an army of men struggles against rock and mud, burning sun and

crippling cold, against the unappeasable strength of the 'Mighty Squaw' (the Columbia River) in flood. The construction engineer Jeff Tunnicliff wonders if 'such a country might conceivably resent the impertinence of temporary little men meddling with its topography, but that was a fanciful idea, unworthy of a construction man'.[54]

In 1941, as work on the Grand Coulee was nearing completion, the Bonneville Power Administration (BPA), who would market the power from the dam, decided to make a documentary film, *The Columbia*, to promote the scheme and public power projects in general. Woody Guthrie was hired to put words and music together for the soundtrack. While the film has faded into obscurity, the songs live on. Guthrie submitted 26 songs to the BPA, and one, 'Roll on, Columbia' ('Roll on Columbia, roll on. Your power is turning our darkness to dawn'), was designated the official Washington State folksong in 1987. It was appropriate that Guthrie, famous at the time for his 'Dust Bowl' ballads about the plight of the Midwest, should have been selected since the dams were part of the New Deal, which not only brought cheap power to rural communities but also gave jobs to those from the Dust Bowl itself. In 'Guys in the Grand Coulee Dam' he describes Old Uncle John Turner and the others (to the tune of the English folksong 'Widdicombe Fair') as:

150-seat wagons transported workers between Hoover Dam and Boulder City.

hard sweatin', hard fightin', hard workin' men,
All along down on Grand Coulee you'll see;
Blasting the canyon and damming her in . . .[55]

'The Grand Coolie [sic] Dam' was also adapted and recorded by Lonnie Donegan in Britain in 1958. The Grand Coulee provided electricity to power the factories that produced aluminium (principally to build aircraft for the war effort); the early Scottish hydro-electric schemes had been built for the same purpose. After the war, the British government, taking a lead from the TVA, set about bringing power production to the Highlands.

The promotion of major development projects often relies on special people, and the harnessing of Scottish water power by a public authority was the brainchild of Tom Johnston. A patriot and Red Clydesider, he had been elected to Parliament as an Independent Labour member in 1922. Although he lost his seat when Ramsay MacDonald's first administration fell in 1924, he was in and out of

An engineers' town built by the Bureau of Reclamation for their staff and families. A model community compared with Grand Coulee town, 'a centre for sin and vice' and known as the 'Cesspool of the New Deal'.

Parliament and government for the next fifteen years. On the outbreak of war in 1939 he was responsible for Civil Defence in Scotland until summoned to Downing Street by Churchill in 1941 to be appointed Secretary of State for Scotland. Johnston accepted on condition that he received no payment for as long as the war lasted. Churchill is recorded as replying, 'Nobody can prevent you taking nothing.'[56] In the words of Emma Wood, Johnston was the political godfather of the North of Scotland Hydro-Electric Board and Churchill the unlikely political sponsor of Britain's first nationalized industry.[57] Between 1945 and 1975 the Board built some 50 dams, 34 of which are on the ICOLD Register of Large Dams. If Johnston was the godfather, the surrogate 'midwife' for the Scottish schemes was James Williamson, who was responsible for the design of many of the early ones, including Loch Sloy, the first buttress dam in Scotland.

The Grand Coulee Dam, Washington.

While dam-building was largely mechanized by the 1930s, in countries where labour was plentiful it could still be used to advantage. At any one time on the fifteen-year construction of the Nagarjunasagar Dam in Andhra Pradesh (completed in 1970), between 30 and 70 thousand labourers worked on the site.

Scheme promotion, however, was often in the hands of single design engineers – with the carrot of designing and overseeing the eventual construction. This was exemplified by Julius Kennard at Cow Green in the 1950s and 1960s. As we shall see, the engineers had to tolerate not only opposition but also interference by their political masters.[58] Scheme promoters didn't always trust their engineers, however; Floyd Dominy, an economics graduate, rose from land development at the US Bureau of Reclamation to Commissioner: 'If Dominy harboured a lifelong grudge, it was

Sheep crossing the Grand Coulee Dam: settlers were allocated farm units, and by 1955 there were 10,000 people living on farms within the project area.

against engineers.'[59] He recognized their 'mystical ability to erect huge structures' but only had faith in his own ability to get them built. He did not have much respect for rivers either, having remarked: 'The unregulated Colorado River is a son of a bitch.'[60] Dominy presided over dozens of big dams, including Glen Canyon, but Marc Reisner maintains that his legacy is 'not so much bricks and mortar as a reputation – a reputation and an attitude. The attitude is his . . . arrogant indifference to sweeping changes in public mood'.[61] Of course, dams are big structures and maybe they need big men to make them real.

From the 1950s the introduction of vibratory rollers for the compaction of concrete, gravel and rock fill advanced the techniques available for dam-building. Embankment dams proliferated from this time[62] since the rollers reduced any settlement. This led to world

Haweswater, Lake District. This 470-metre-long dam is unusual, being a concrete buttress dam, but the 44 buttresses are widened at their end so that the dam's air face, while appearing uniform, is in fact hollow, comprising a series of linked pyramid chambers, thus saving concrete.

records in dam-building: the Tarbela Dam (1976) on the Indus in Pakistan (at 105 million cubic metres, the record for embankment volume) and the Nurek Dam (1980) in Tajikistan (at 300 metres the tallest dam in the world). An even taller rock-fill dam, the Rogun, also in Tajikistan, was started in 1976 but was stalled on the break-up of the USSR and then destroyed in a flood in 1993. A deal was signed with RUSAL, the Russian aluminium producer, in 2004 to complete the Rogun in order to power the aluminium smelter that RUSAL is hoping to build. It will be 335 metres high when complete. The dams of Tajikistan have been somewhat controversial in that they have the potential to starve neighbours such as Uzbekistan, Turkmenistan and Kazakstan of water, as well as turning off the tap to the rapidly depleting Aral Sea.

This chapter has been principally about the designers and builders of dams, but the story would not have been complete without reference to technical advances introduced by engineers. Dam projects are now so big that no one person can be identified as being the 'dam engineer'. Ever since the Six Companies combined to tender for Hoover Dam in 1931, consortia have grown, and the creative engineer has been lost in a sea of anonymity. Even consultancies which still bore the names of their famous founders — Binnies, Babtie, Hawksley, Rofe and Kennard — have been swallowed up by international organizations in recent years. Now even these are but cogs in the wheel of larger project funders and development corporations — the Three Gorges Dam will cost $25 billion when complete. We may well ask, 'What do these organizations or governments care about the beauty of their dams?' This is the subject of the next chapter.

3 Dam Beauty and Dam Proud

If you seek his monument, look about you . . .
Inscription to Hermann Schussler,
Crystal Springs Dam, San Mateo, California

As Louis Sullivan maintained, form should follow function for most structures, but in the case of dams it could be said that form follows *location* — topography, geology, materials or locality. Perhaps the Shaker principle that 'beauty arises from practicality' would be more appropriate for dams because they *can* indeed be things of beauty. In this chapter the dam as a thing of beauty – a thing that generates or instils pride – will be explored.

William Hogarth, writing in 1753, reflected on the work of artists and landscape designers, looking to nature rather than art to set the standard for beauty.[1] He considered that 'straight lines are dull since they vary only in length; a waving line on the contrary — the line of beauty — has two curves . . . '[2] At its simplest, this 'line of beauty' was an elongated S and can be seen in plan of the main dam at Stourhead, which, although planned in 1744, was not completed until 1754,[3] so after the publication of Hogarth's work. It is suggested therefore that, if engineers were concerned with beauty, they had precedents to look to in the world of landscape design.

Dams are probably at their best when following a curved profile in plan or perspective. Straight buttress dams do not necessarily make a positive contribution to the pastoral scene, though of course beauty may be in the eyes of the designer as well as the beholder. As

Sir Robert Farquhar said in his objection to the Thirlmere Dam in the Lake District in 1879, 'There is no accounting for Tastes. Dr Johnson is said to have been fond of plum pudding with lobster sauce and the pleasures of the eye may perhaps vary as much as those of the palate.'[4] The American photojournalist Margaret Bourke-White, who photographed industrial subjects around the world, including Hoover Dam and the power plant at Niagara Falls in addition to the Fort Peck Dam whose photograph graced *Life*'s inaugural cover, said 'dynamos are more beautiful to me than pearls.'[5]

The poet William Shenstone coined the term 'landscape garden' to describe the English advocacy of the 'natural' look on the estates of country houses. By the mid-eighteenth century, parks were being designed by William Kent, 'Capability' Brown and Humphry Repton. They introduced the serpentine lakes (the line of beauty in three dimensions), avenues, clumps of trees and grottoes immortalized by Alexander Pope in his 'Epistle to Lord Burlington' (1731):

> To build, to plant whatever you intend . . .
> To swell the terras, or to sink the Grot;
> In all, let Nature never be forgot.
> Consult the Genius of the Place in all . . .

Buttress dam on the River Vire, Normandy. Wadsworth would maintain that too much repetition with equal spacing is not easy on the eye.

Wealthy municipalities went into the countryside, purchased tracts of land and laid them out to collect as much water as possible.[10] This approach produced some dramatic contrasts which developed either from operational requirements or from deliberate aesthetic policy. Tom Turner described this as the *innovative* approach to design. New reservoirs were designed to contrast with their surroundings with dams designed in Greek or baronial styles. Since the 1960s, however, again according to Turner, reservoirs have been subject to *conservation* design to make them look as natural as possible and to integrate them with the landscape.[11]

In Britain after the war, dams were often constructed entirely of concrete, especially as its quality improved and masonry work became more expensive.[12] One of the last masonry-faced concrete dams is at Claerwen. Designed in the 1930s to reflect the design of the other dams in the Elan Valley scheme, it was finally built in 1952. The use of concrete gave engineers the opportunity to be more

Concrete blockwork and spillway for the 1000-m-long embankment Derwent Dam on the border between Durham and Northumberland, opened in 1967.

creative with details but at the same time challenged them; it might have been more straightforward to design and build with massive blocks of granite in rugged countryside.

The first use of concrete for dams since the Roman period was at Boyds Corner Dam for the water supply of New York in 1872, at the same time as it was used in the building of the hydroelectricity dam at Pérolles near Berne in Switzerland. In 1890, using interlocking concrete blocks, the Swiss-born Hermann Schussler built the massive 45-metre-tall curved gravity Crystal Springs Dam for the water supply of San Francisco. With an S-shaped roadway running along its crest, Crystal Springs almost personifies Hogarth's line of beauty, but it is more notable for withstanding the 1906 San Francisco earthquake. The construction method therefore recommended itself to the designers of Hoover Dam more than 40 years later.

Concrete offered great opportunities for designers, and, after John S. Eastwood and his 'ultimate' multiple-arch buttress dam, the US

Crystal Springs curved gravity concrete dam at San Mateo, California, completed in 1890 to supply water for San Francisco.

Indian Service built the 76-metre-high multiple-dome reinforced-concrete Coolidge Dam in 1928. It derives its strength against crushing in much the same way as an egg; the Art Deco form is an extreme example of the use of a cupola. The Coolidge Dam is also remarkable since it was built to provide irrigation water for the San Carlos Indian Reservation in southern Arizona. The work of the Indian Service was overshadowed by its big brother, the Bureau of Reclamation, but at the time it was making considerable contributions to the promotion of Native American agriculture in the West.[13] The form of the Coolidge Dam was replicated at the Daniel Johnson multiple-arch hydroelectric dam in Quebec, completed in 1970 to the design of André Coyne. At 214 metres it is the tallest multiple-arch concrete dam in the world and demonstrates how variation can bring interest to repetitive buttresses.

In 1929, Charles Fowler, who had been lecturing on the subject of engineering architecture at the University of Washington at Seattle,

The three egg-shaped domes and buttresses of the reinforced concrete Coolidge Dam, Arizona, completed in 1928 by the Bureau of Indian Affairs.

sought to set out the case for it to be treated as an art form in his *Ideals of Engineering Architecture*.[14] Unusually, he made specific reference to dams and beauty: 'the greatest curve is on the downstream face, which is a fundamental element of beauty, and when the dam is arched horizontally, the artistic appearance is still more enhanced.' One of his examples was the Roosevelt Dam in Arizona – 'it is curved in plan with a radius of 400ft, and has a curved face downstream, so that basically it is very pleasing in appearance. The ornamental pilastered crest is also very nicely detailed, and illustrates what a small additional cost is necessary to add some artistic features'. The attractiveness of this dam is confirmed by its use in several advertising campaigns, as we have seen.

Fowler particularly approved of the O'Shaughnessy Dam in Yosemite: 'the structure is the most remarkable one of its kind in the world, where simplicity has been the keynote to beauty, and to harmony with the mountain masses.' Have our views changed in 75 years, or is there a case for retaining this dam about which there was so much controversy in the nineteenth century and which is proposed for removal by some in the twenty-first? Fowler also extolled the virtues of the new Croton Dam for New York as 'one of the finest

André Coyne's multiple-arch Daniel Johnson Dam on the Manicouagan River, Québec, completed in 1970. The owners, HydroQuebec, proclaim, 'Let yourself be mesmerized!'

there was no need for planning permission or conditions.[32] Wimbleball Reservoir, built between 1975 and 1979 in Exmoor National Park, was provided with a pink tinge to its concrete dam, and 12,000 trees were planted 'since attention was required to the environmental impact'.[33] It may be questioned whether such a distinctive structure really needed such treatment.

A picture emerges in the post-war design of dams and reservoirs that is similar in some respects to that of the previous hundred years. The design of dams was largely undertaken by a handful of engineers, but, with all the pressures that have been described, design teams were extended to include landscape architects. Again, the design work appears to have been concentrated in just a few practices. History will judge whether this approach resulted in 'beautiful' dams, but the Megget Reservoir being selected by the viewing public for a design award was undoubtedly a tribute to the landscape advice of Cairns & Partners.

Wimbleball Dam, Exmoor National Park, a mass concrete diamond-head buttress dam.

Brenda Colvin, writing in 1947, advised that 'small, natural dams forming a chain of pools along valleys are better than very large dams . . . [with] modelling of the ground forms to flow into existing contours, rather than uniform slopes and rigid lines'.[34] She had particular advice for the burgeoning reservoirs 'near the A30 at Staines . . . if enough space is available around the brink to allow for pleasing modelling of the contours . . . if the space is limited to the engineering necessities the steep straight banks are ugly'.[35] This advice was further developed in 1956 by Sylvia Crowe, who claimed that it was possible for dams and reservoirs 'to find a place in the wild landscape by the sheer deception of appearing as natural lakes . . . [giving a landscape] of magnificent composition'.[36] Her theme was that efforts could and should be made to seek the blending of reservoirs into the receiving environment to give the appearance of naturalness. Crowe was echoing the words of Colvin when describing the London reservoirs – this time in the Lea Valley – as 'a liability [rather] than an asset to the landscape'.[37] Again, she advocated contouring the 'steep, harsh, and bare' embankments out into the surrounding ground where planting could take place away from the clay bank. She made the point that reservoirs should not of 'necessity detract from the visual composition of a scene . . . it is only by misuse of their potentialities that they so often spoil a scene which they should enhance. Ironically, some of the worst offences are committed in a misguided attempt at amenity'.[38]

Turner[39] included a list of questions which landscape architects should ask in the planning of a reservoir, including: Is it designed to be similar to or different from its surroundings? How will it improve the scenery and contribute to the creation of new habitats and improve opportunities for outdoor recreation? At the conclusion of the twentieth century, *Water Supply*[40] dropped the rather condescending to enrich ploughland. We shall compel it!'[45] Clearly there was competition to extract the greatest kudos and pride, as well as power, from the Dnieper.

Begun in 1928, the contrast in construction techniques between the Dneprovsk and the Volkhovstroi could not be more stark. Proclaimed as the success of the Soviet Union (when in fact it mirrored a worldwide phenomenon), an enormous army of peasant diggers and horses and carts had been replaced by excavators, railways and electric and steam cranes. There was another dimension to the construction, however: D. Saslavsky, writing in 1932, maintained that the West was feeling threatened by the growth of the Soviet Union: the

> imperialist world sought to undermine the Soviet efforts – bourgeois engineering intelligentsia infiltrated the design team and attempted to sabotage the plans to hamper the development of the electrical engineering industry in the USSR . . . however, the Soviet government, supported by the working class turned the tables and quashed the hostile intrigues of the counter-revolutionaries.

He went on to say that 'The Dnieprostroi accomplished miracles of which the engineering world speaks in amazement.'[46]

To the novelist Anna Louise Strong, writing *Wild River* in 1943, the Dneprovsk was 'the electric heart of the Ukraine', but, as its generators had been manufacted by General Electric, she saw it as having 'united the engineering skill of . . . two countries'.[47] This 60-metre-high, 760-metre-wide gravity dam was completed in 1932 but was destroyed by the retreating Soviet army in 1941 and in turn by the retreating Germans in 1943. Rebuilt after the war, it was back to full power production by 1950; a second powerhouse was added in 1980.

The Rogun (when completed) and the Nurek rock- and earth-fill dams are today the first and second highest in the world, while the Inguri concrete arch dam is fourth. St Petersburg is defended from flooding from the Gulf of Finland by a surge barrier similar to the Thames Barrier and the Ijssel barrier in Holland but is more than 25 kilometres long. The Bratsk earth-fill and gravity dam in Siberia caused a sensation when it was built in 1967, not only for its sheer size (125 metres high and nearly 5 kilometres long) and its hydropower capacity (twice that of Grand Coulee) but also because

'Communism equals Soviet Power and Electrification': Lenin's dream realized by the Dneiper Dam, 1932.

of the enormity of the construction task. It is situated in the taiga, where the temperature remains below zero for most of the year, falling to as low as –60 °C.[48] The author and playwright Alan Sillitoe, writing in 1964, confessed that he had never been impressed by the size of anything until he saw the Bratsk Dam. A new city was founded at Bratsk in 1955, and – once women were encouraged to settle there – it gained the highest birth rate in the Soviet Union. Sillitoe suggested that 'dams are the new fertility symbols of the modern age' (from a village of 2,500 residents in 1948, today Bratsk is an industrial city with a population of more than 300,000). He saw the Bratsk Dam as a 'twentieth century monument to the great atheist-materialists of the Russian Revolution'.[49]

However, many Soviet projects came to a halt in 1991, the Rogun among them. After 1945, the USSR not only built large dams for itself but elsewhere in the world, for example the High Dam at Aswan in Egypt. The Russian approach to design was summed up by V. M. Serebryanskii: 'The development of the architectural form of any dam should be subordinate to an expression of the functions satisfied by that dam'[50] – a more brutal expression of the advice to students offered by Gosschalk!

We have seen that dams have often been neglected or forgotten: once built they do tend to quietly get on with their job. However, if built large enough they can be a source of pride for any nation. It is apparent from First Day Covers sent in Japan in the 1950s that the Japanese were also proud of (and perhaps promoting) their reconstruction programme. The 140-metre-high Sakuma Dam on the River Tenryu, begun in 1952, was completed in 1956 to generate electricity; the Ogochi Dam was completed in the following year to provide Tokyo's water supply. As Roland A. Wank put it when speaking of the TVA, such projects are 'expressive of the pride a whole nation takes in itself'.[51]

At the inauguration of the construction of the Bhakra Dam and Nangal Canal in the Punjab in 1954, Prime Minister Nehru expressed his awe through nationalism mixed with religious reverence:

A magnificent work . . . which only that nation can take up which has

Japanese First Day Covers celebrating the Sakuma and Ogochi Dams.

faith and boldness! . . . it has become a symbol of a nation's will to march forward with strength, determination and courage . . . the biggest temple and mosque and *gurdwara* is the place where man works for the good of mankind. Which place can be greater than this, this Bhakra-Nangal? Where can be a greater and holier place than this?[52]

However, just four years later Nehru had a change of heart. Speaking to the Central Board of Irrigation and Power in November 1958, he deplored this 'disease of giganticism – the idea of doing big under-takings . . . for the sake of showing that we can do [them] is not a good outlook at all'.[53] By this time, he was favouring small irrigation and power projects as being far less disruptive in respect of social upheaval. These thoughts came in the evening of Nehru's life and before the anti-dam movements of the 1970s. However, they came too late to reverse a course already set.[54]

Patrick McCully described dams as

much more than simple machines to generate electricity and store water. They are concrete, rock and earth expressions of the dominant ideology of the technological age: icons of economic development and scientific progress to match nuclear bombs and motor cars. The builders of Hoover were advised by an architect to strip the dam of planned ornamentation in order to accentuate the visual power of its colossal concrete face.[55]

He quotes Theodore Steinberg, a historian at the University of Michigan, as saying that Hoover Dam 'was supposed to signify great-ness, power and domination. It was planned that way'.[56]

On 23 June 1896, some 90 members of the Woolhope Naturalists Field Club visited the works of the 'proposed Birmingham Water Supply'. A report of the visit made by H. C. Moore is recorded in the club's annual journal. Moore noted that the question was asked, 'How can a visit to engineering works of man be comprehended within the scope of a Naturalists' Field Club?' He responded, 'It is the duty of . . . society . . . to trace the triumphant art of the engineer in storing up in abundance such an essential to our daily life as water.'[57] More recent writers have even suggested that dams can and should enhance scenic beauty.[58]

For an exploration of beauty which derives from the simple functionality of dams, we can look in some detail at that icon of American pride (in its economic and technical competence), the Hoover Dam. If asked to name a dam at random, most respondents would say, 'Hoover Dam', and it is worth considering why this particular one out of the 45,000 large dams in the world should have become such an icon. In 1981, the Hoover Dam was listed on the US National Register of Historic Places, and in 1985 it was designated a National Historic Landmark. In the view of Carl Reisner, it marked the beginning of the Age of Dams. As Franklin D. Roosevelt had said in his 1935 inauguration address, 'I came, I saw, and I was conquered.' Wallace Stegner, the American historian, novelist and environmentalist, wrote, 'It is certainly one of the world's wonders, that sweeping cliff of concrete . . . everything about the dam is marked by the immense smooth efficient beauty that seems peculiarly American.'[59]

William Wattis, President of the Six Companies contracted to build the Hoover Dam, called it 'just a dam, but it's a damn big dam'. It was to be 'a colossus: the biggest undertaking in which the US Government had ever been involved'.[60] On completion, as 'Lake Mead started to fill behind the dam . . . a flood which would have deluged the farmland of the Imperial Valley was now controlled, and the river's good behaviour extended into providing water in the season of drought which came later. The Colorado was at last subdued to man's will'.[61] As Donald Worster has said, 'the Wild West was tamed not by the six-gun but by the impounded waters of wild rivers.' Roosevelt saw this transformation as a 'twentieth century marvel . . .'[62] All the dimensions are superlative [and] represent and embody the accumulated engineering knowledge and experience of centuries'. The dam 'became a trophy for the nation and although larger dams have since been built, not one could usurp the special position it holds'.[63]

The dam originally planned for Boulder Canyon on the border of Arizona and Nevada was relocated to Black Canyon for better impoundment but remained known as Boulder Dam. At the official start of the project, 17 September 1930, it was announced that its name would be changed in honour of the President who had made it possible. However, in 1932 Hoover lost the election to Franklin Roosevelt; in 1933 a memorandum was issued to the Bureau of Reclamation that the dam should again be referred to by its original name. All official promotional and tourist materials now called it Boulder Dam. However, after Roosevelt died in 1945, President Harry Truman signed a law reinstating the name 'Hoover Dam'.

Technical features were determined by the Bureau's engineering staff, overseen by John Savage, but the Moderne style was the work of Gordon B. Kaufmann, a Los Angeles architect who had never before designed a large-scale engineering project.[64] However, he had received the commission in 1931 to design the Los Angeles Times Building from newspaper publisher Harry Chandler, who happened to be a strong supporter of the dam.[65]

Kaufmann had been born in London and trained at London Polytechnic and the Royal College of Art. He had emigrated to Canada in 1910 and moved to Southern California in 1913. He set up his own architectural practice in 1924, and by the 1930s his style was very much in the Art Deco mould, exhibiting a 'simplification of design and adoption of modernistic stylistic images, while still retaining vestiges of ornament and plastic modelling'.[66] He wrote, 'There was never any desire or attempt to create an architectural effect or style, but rather to take each problem and integrate it to the whole in order to secure a system of plain surfaces relieved by shadows here and there where the plan or requirements suggested'.[67]

Richard Guy Wilson suggested that Kaufmann was influenced by such Los Angeles 'avant-garde' architects as Rudolph Schindler and Richard Neutra, as well as by Modernist sources such as the French architect Tony Garnier and the Italian Futurist Antonio Sant' Elia. He also likened Kaufmann's work to a film set, citing Fritz Lang's *Metropolis* (1927). Wilson described the original engineering drawings of 1930 from the Bureau; when compared with Kaufmann's sketches of 1933, his influence is apparent. Where the Bureau had a balustrade and access towers (topped with two enormous eagles) as attachments to the dam face, Kaufmann integrated the towers such that they are continuations of the dam face. (In this he was following the edict of John Rennie: 'the works of the engineer . . . must strike by their mass and proportion rather than by trifling details and minutiae of ornament'.[68]) The entrances to the towers have two large cast-concrete panels by the sculptor Oskar J. W. Hansen, depicting flood control, irrigation, power and the history of the area. The low relief, semi-classical cubistic style typified Art Deco.[69] The intake towers had originally been crenellated with what Wilson described as a Crown of Thorns; Kaufmann amended this to create a cap with vertical buttresses including internal lighting so that at night it 'conveyed an almost supernatural effect as if some hidden dynamo was pulsating energy'.[70] He also tried to provide a gradation of colour from dark red at the base to lighter red at the top by varying the curing time of the concrete. In this he was unsuccessful, and today, in the glare of the

Antonio Sant' Elia, *Electric Power Plant*, 1914, ink and pencil on paper.

Original artist's impression for Boulder (Hoover) Dam, on the Arizona–Nevada border.

Hoover Dam: intake towers.

desert sun, the structure appears to be a wall of white against the rose-pink rocks.

Kaufmann recommended a Denver artist, Allen True, to advise on colour for the interior of the plant. True said that it should 'express through architectural planning the new understanding of functional form and satisfy in every respect the pride and esthetic joy that man finds in his accomplishments'.[71] We find lobbies inside the towers with floors of polished dark green and black terrazzo and with walls in marble of the same colour scheme. The heavy bronze doors open on to decorative terrazzo panels in the floor based on South-west Indian motifs from baskets, bowls and sand paintings. For the turbine hall True selected ten Native American colours but 'as brilliant as possible'. So the generators are deep red, while the gantries are jade green with vermilion, blue and yellow valves. Together with a plethora of shiny steel panels, switches and dials, the whole offers 'a far more dramatic setting than even Fritz Lang could have conceived'.[72] (However, Lang would probably not have included the Union flag).

Hansen also won a competition to design a monument to celebrate the dam – the winged figures illustrated on page 11. The two ten-metre-tall 'Winged figures of the Republic' seated on polished black diorite are made of bronze and 'symbolize the universal aspirations of mankind and the achievement of Americans'. Hansen intended their 'stoic visages, with the look of eagles to represent those who settled the West'.[73] 'The building of Hoover Dam', he continued, 'belongs to the sagas of the daring . . . [and] the bronzes . . . symbolize the readiness for defense of our institutions.'[74] Each figure weighed 4 tons, and the diorite bases were placed on blocks of ice and slowly lowered into their precise position as the ice melted to prevent damage to them.

The Hoover Dam belies one of the myths of Modern architecture as proposed by Le Corbusier and others, that the great functional structures were simply the work of engineers. Kaufmann – an architect – converted the dam's design from 'a banal, warmed-over classicism style to the realm of modernism'.[75] Artists and photographers including Ansel Adams have tried to capture the structure's nascent power on paper, and writers have seen it as a symbol of the new, modern world of special beauty. In 1937 J. B. Priestley saw 'that world we catch a glimpse of in . . . H. G. Wells' film 'Things to Come', a world of giant machines and titanic communal enterprises'.[76] For Joan Didion, in her 1979 novel *The White Album*, the dam is a tomorrow that never came. She cannot get it out of her head: 'the dam will materialize, its pristine concave face gleaming white against the harsh rusts . . . of that rock canyon.'[77]

Hoover Dam photographed by Ansel Adams in 1941.

However, it would be ironic if Kaufmann had indeed been influenced by Sant' Elia. In his *Manifesto of Futurist Architecture*, the Italian city planner launched an assault on past and present practice, seeking new materials and, more importantly, patterns of life. This young Milanese envisaged the redevelopment of a new city, *La Città Nuova*, symbolic of a new age that looked towards America rather than Europe for inspiration. However, this Futurist city required control within a quasi-totalitarian social structure at odds with the free spirit of the American dream.[78] Donald Worster saw the Hoover Dam as a 'study in domination', so perhaps the association is not so tenuous.

Hoover Dam: turbine hall.

The Bureau of Reclamation, in a publicity film in the 1930s, called the building of 'Boulder' Dam the story of the fruition of humanity's plans to break the will of a treacherous and tempestuous river, to tame it and harness its floods to serve the ends and purposes of progressive civilization – a 'drama of conquest', an 'ambition to conquer and control' and 'man's conquest'.[79] Fine words. Forty years later, Didion imagined the world without humanity, with only the dam left: 'a dynamo finally free of man, splendid at last in its absolute isolation, transmitting power and releasing water to a world where no one is'.[80] Worster disagreed, seeing human domination over nature as 'quite simply an illusion . . . Do what we will, the Colorado will one day find an unimpeded way to the sea'.[81]

Whatever else the Hoover Dam stands for, it is surely one of the most beautiful structures produced by the human hand and brain, and may be fairly compared to other twentieth-century creations such as the Millau Viaduct, the Sydney Opera House and Concorde. It has a gracefulness in its clean, curved lines (almost a 'line of beauty') of a scale appropriate to its setting, and yet it is not afraid to state its function. It had only twenty years as the tallest dam in the world but established itself in that time as a wonder of the world and is now confirmed as a 'must see' on tourist itineraries.

In 1957 it was overtaken in terms of scale by the Mauvoisin arch dam (250 metres) and then, in 1961, by the Grande Dixence (285 metres) gravity dam, both in Switzerland. (The Vaiont arch dam [262 metres] in Italy was also completed in 1961 but was overwhelmed by a rock slide in 1963, as we shall see.) Still in Switzerland, a dam Schnitter called 'outstanding in respect of both originality and elegance' is the Hongrin twin-arch dam 30 kilometres east of Lausanne.[82] Designed by H. Gicot, it was completed in 1969 and comprises two arches 125 and 90 metres high respectively which meet at a common thrust block. While the Swiss engineers looked to the

American experience after the war to provide construction ideas, there was 'little that could be learned from the USA in the shaping of concrete dams'.[83] Schnitter claimed that no detrimental effects on the environment have been encountered by Swiss dams, although there have been important changes in the landscape. In his opinion, whether a 'reservoir defaces or enriches a landscape is . . . mainly a question of taste about which no dispute is said to be possible'.[84]

The arch was discovered by the Sumerians in the Euphrates Valley in 3500 BC, when they assembled stones to work in compression rather than bending as in a beam. For dams the compressive force should be uniform, and the most appropriate arch form is of variable curvature, decreasing from the key to the spring line. In other words, a dam in plan should be elliptical or parabolic – as at Hongrin – rather than circular.[85] In fact most arch dams are circular in plan with the exception of those in Switzerland, which are mostly of variable radius.

Tastes vary, of course, and whether these dams embody a kind of beauty must be judged by the individual. A scheme for the 96-metre-high Zakarias concrete arch dam in the Tafjord Valley in north-western Norway demonstrates that at least some people regard them as beautiful. The Zakarias has won several design and construction awards. Described by its investor as 'total madness', he plans to build a 40-bedroom hotel on top of the dam so that visitors can 'experience the tension and silence of this special place'.[86]

The style of dam-building has changed from monumentalism and pride to conservation and (almost) apology. Economy and environmentalism may have robbed us of the opportunity to be adventurous. Perhaps we need the likes of Roberto Calatrava to bring his (or her) imagination to bear on the design of dams. There can be a place for earth-embankment dams, but the exploration of stunning design should not be sacrificed for anything but safety. What happens if safety is not given priority is the subject of the next chapter.

Proposals for an art gallery and hotel on the Zakarias Dam in Norway.

4 | Dam Failure

I wish this dam would break and flood this awful town . . .
Sideshow Bob (*The Simpsons*)

James Thurber claimed, in 'The Day the Dam Broke', that there are few alarms in the world more terrifying than 'The dam has broken!'[1] However, given the many hundreds of thousands of dams that have been built throughout the world over the centuries, this siren call has been heard relatively infrequently. (Ironically, Thurber's was a false alarm.) Indeed, since 1900 (an era during which dam construction has known few bounds) there have been only a hundred or so breaks in the structures of large dams – most caused by overtopping in times of flood.[2] In this respect, earth dams have been particularly vulnerable, with their empirical design standards – when there were any – being unreliable until the twentieth century. This safety record speaks volumes for the skill (perhaps along with some luck) of designers and builders, especially when compared with natural disasters. However, if humans intervene with nature, they have to be held responsible for their actions. The inhabitants of San Francisco may have been excused for not realizing they were set-tling in an earthquake zone when 450 people lost their lives in 1906; excuses were *not* acceptable when the St Francis (i.e. San Francisco) Dam, built on a geological fault line to the north of Los Angeles, col-lapsed in 1928, drowning roughly the same number. Having said that, to the designers' credit, the San Mateo concrete dam, built between 1887 and 1889, survived the 1906 San Francisco earthquake. Dam failure none the less remains one of our greatest fears. In 'The Afghan', Frederick Forsyth describes a suspected terrorist 'singing' under interrogation as 'like watching the Boulder [sic] Dam give way'.[3]

The decade between 1920 and 1930 was the last time that an appreciable number of dams failed – mostly in Britain, Italy and the US – and consequently legislation was effected which, in association with an improved understanding of dam engineering, led to a commensurate improvement in reliability. Whatever else might be true, Norman Smith maintained that the benefits of dams have become available at little risk to life or property.[4]

It is not only poor design, construction, accident or neglect which leads to the collapse of dams, however, and, on occasion, their destruction has been deliberate.

Methods and measures to control the Nile in recent times are described elsewhere, but dams were built from about 2600 BC to protect Cairo from annual floods. The dam at Memphis, 20 kilometres south of Cairo, at the beginning of the 'Pyramid Age' was 14 metres high and 113 metres long. Construction is estimated to have taken up to ten years and consisted of placing 17,000 stone revetment blocks, each weighing 300 kilograms, on the dam's faces to protect the core of sand and gravel. Nicholas Schnitter considered that it must have been breached several times during construction (rather like Periyar in the nineteenth century) by the very floods it was designed to control, and that this put off Egyptian engineers from building dams for another 800 years.[5] The Sabaeans in Yemen had been damming their river, the Danah, since 1500 BC and built a great dam in about 500 BC some 20 metres high and 700 metres long. It had an inadequate spillway and was regularly breached by floods until, after some 1,200 years, the final failure was recorded in the Koran: 'But they [the Sabaeans] turned aside from the obedience of Allah: so we sent upon them the flood of Iram and changed their gardens into those of bitter fruit and tamarisk.' The 50,000 people whose livelihoods depended on the dam emigrated, never to return.

The Romans learned that insufficient spillway capacity could cause dam failure following the collapse of the Alcantrilla Dam at Toledo in Spain in AD 100. An early example of an English dam being breached in modern times was the 11-metre-high Blackbrook earth dam, built between 1795 and 1797 for the Charnwood Forest Canal on the Leicester Navigation. It was breached first in 1799 due to snow melt overtopping the crest; having been repaired, the same thing happened again, resulting in the canal – which was in some commercial difficulties by this time – being abandoned. The dam was designed by William Jessop with a central puddle-clay core; both faces had slopes of 1:1.7. More than a hundred years later, in 1906, a third attempt was made to build a dam at the site – this time successfully but only just. A masonry gravity dam was built to supply Loughborough with water, and the engineers were able to examine the construction of the old earth dam. This confirmed that it was of unsound construction – soil had been used as a core just 0.75 m into a trench, and the embankments comprised rock and soil – but Jessop cannot be blamed since he had only recommended the construction of the dam and ceased employment with the Navigation on 4 June 1795. The resident engineer, Charles Staveley, then took over, and although a clay core had been specified by Jessop the construction was not carried out to his specifications. There was further drama when in 1957 the parapet wall of this dam was cracked and dislodged by an earthquake – a very unusual occurrence in England!

Dams built for irrigation purposes in Spain at about the same time suffered a similar fate. The 50-metre-high Puentes Dam near

Murcia in southern Spain was built in 1791 on alluvial foundations which had been washed away by a flood in 1648. It was surprising that the same site was retained, but this time the designer, Géronimo Martínez de Lara, had the dam founded on wooden piles driven into the river's alluvium. It took until 1802 for the reservoir to fill, which then resulted in a washout of the alluvium forming an 18 by 34 metre hole in the dam. More than a thousand people drowned in the city of Lorca and surrounding areas in the ensuing flood. In 1881−4 a further, this time successful, attempt was made to build a dam at Puentes but on a rock outcrop 200 metres downstream from the original site.

Other British navigation dams were damaged by floods at the turn of the nineteenth century. The 14-metre Diggle embankment dam was breached in 1799 and 1806 but replaced by a new dam upstream in 1830, while the 13-metre Tunnel End Dam was damaged in 1799 by floods and also rebuilt in 1806.

In 1850 the Woodhead Dam, part of the Longendale water-supply scheme for Manchester, collapsed, most likely due to water percolating through the grits beneath it. The Bilberry Dam south of Huddersfield in Yorkshire, built on similar foundations, collapsed in 1852. It had been promoted by a group of mill owners to conserve water during summer low flows in the rivers Holme and Colne draining from the Yorkshire Pennines. Their scheme involved a total of eight regulating reservoirs, and they received Royal Assent in June 1837. This set up the Holme Reservoirs Commission with the power to raise £40,000 by subscription. The first three dams were to be more than 20 metres high at a time when there were only seven higher dams in the whole of the UK. As Geoffrey Binnie, the water engineer and historian, wrote in amazement, 'This extraordinarily ambitious project . . . [was] undertaken by a group of technically ignorant and inexperienced men with limited financial resources.'[6]

Being short of money as well as water, the Commissioners did not appoint an engineer to advise on the siting of the dams. Instead, the engineer George Leather was engaged to prepare designs on the pre-determined alignment, prepare specifications to invite tenders from contractors and, rather than supervise construction, 'come over now and then as circumstances might require'. Given that there was no railway from Leeds, where Leather had his offices, a site visit would have meant him being away for the best part of three days – time he could no doubt ill afford. He may have been relieved not to have to make the journey, but perhaps did not realize the difficulty of building earth dams – of which he had little experience; he didn't visit the site during the critical first two years of construction. The tenders were prepared at the beginning of October 1838 and were let before the end of the month – an indication of the haste propelling the Commissioners to disaster.

Bilberry was to be 20 metres high with a puddle-clay core wall extending below ground level. Sharps, the contractors, started work in early 1839, but the dam leaked from the beginning and their contract was terminated in 1843. From then until 1845 a second contractor, David Porter, was engaged. His efforts to stop the leaks were unsuccessful, and, regrettably, the dam was left to its own devices until one o'clock in the morning of 5 February 1852 after heavy rainfall, 'the ponderous embankment, with a roar as loud as a peal of thunder, burst outwards, and the pent-up waters escaped on their mission of death and desolation',[7] drowning 80 people and causing considerable destruction, including the loss of more than 20 mills in Holmfirth nearly 5 kilometres downstream.

At the ensuing inquest, it became clear that a spring had been encountered in the cut-off trench excavation and the puddle clay was in constant contact with water. Porter recounted in his evidence that 'instead of a stiff puddle, it was all sludge', and the embank-

ment settled 6 to 7 centimetres each morning. A second Bill had been prepared in 1846 to repeal the existing 1837 Act and to authorize the borrowing of sufficient capital to repair the dam. J. F. La Trobe Bateman and George Leather were both asked to estimate for the necessary repair works; Bateman estimated £2,900 while Leather, realizing the major work required, estimated £7,800. In the event the Bill was not proceeded with. The Commissioners were advised to lower the height of the overflow so as to reduce pressure on the dam, but when preparations were made, they changed their mind, allowing their commercial interests 'to overcome prudence and their duty to the general public'.[8]

The Government Inspector, Capt. R. C. Moody (previously a Professor at the Royal Military Academy and the first Governor of the Falkland Islands), at the time the Commanding Royal Engineer at Newcastle, asserted in his evidence that a puddle wall should keep the whole watertight, with the heaviest portion of embankment materials on the outside and the more binding materials on the inside and well rammed. (This advice became standard practice in

Bilberry Reservoir, Holmfirth, Yorkshire, created by mill-owners 'for the purpose of treasuring up the water which runs so abundantly in these mountainous districts'.

Britain twelve years later, after a second dam failure, and no earth dams with clay cores have failed since. Moody observed that this was not the case at Bilberry: the embankment material was very loose, and the fact that the puddle was in contact with the spring had caused it progressively to collapse.

The jury found that the reservoir was defective in its original construction and that the Commissioners, engineer and overseer were culpable in not securing the proper regulation of the works; the Commissioners were also guilty of permitting the reservoir to remain in a dangerous state. As a result of the disaster, an Act of Parliament of 1863 permitted complaints to be made to magistrates on the safety of reservoirs, but it was not to be until 1930 that the Reservoirs (Safety Provisions) Act was passed.

George Leather retired three years later, and when he died in 1870 there was only a brief announcement in the *Leeds Mercury* that made no mention of his achievements; his career ended in obscurity. As we shall see, however, his family's association with failed dams was not over.

Capt. Moody also recommended that the Commissioners appoint an engineer to make the necessary reparations. The Holme Reservoirs Act finally received Royal Assent in 1853 with J. F. La Trobe Bateman named as Engineer, with funds authorized for the rebuild and the replacement of the Commissioners by a new board of directors. In 1854 a new contract was let in the sum of £5,500 for Bilberry to be rebuilt on the same site but 10 metres upstream. In fact Bateman's proposals were similar to those of Leather; in 1867, Bateman extended the spillway.

Following the Reservoirs (Safety Provisions) Act 1930, periodic inspections of the rebuilt dam in 1933 and 1943 detected a variable flow in a culvert beneath it, leaving the inspectors to assume that there was a spring under the embankment. This was in fact the same spring that had caused the problem with the clay core in the first place, but it had been diverted into a culvert by Bateman. In 1937, Huddersfield Corporation obtained an Act to create a new reservoir at Digley just downstream from Bilberry, but construction was postponed by the war. On 29 May 1944 a devastating storm hit the valley, causing considerable destruction in Holmfirth and the loss of three lives. Part of the embankment was washed away, but the dam held – a testimony to Bateman's work. In 1954, the Digley Reservoir was built, submerging much of the old Bilberry embankment such that Bilberry Reservoir now merely acts as a large silt trap.

The most serious dam failure in Britain occurred at Dale Dyke (Bradfield) near Sheffield in 1864; John Towlerton Leather, who had served his apprenticeship under his uncle George, was the engineer. The dam was built for the Sheffield Waterworks Company and was 29 metres high and 380 metres long at its crest – a large embankment for its time. It had a clay core 20 metres below ground level against which shale and rubble were placed. Construction started in January 1859; progress was slow, and filling started in June 1863.

Dale Dyke Dam, near Sheffield. The collapse of 1864 as sketched for *The Illustrated London News*.

By 10 March 1864 the water level was just below the overflow weir and still rising. The following afternoon a horizontal crack was seen near the crest of the dam, and at 11.30 p.m. on 11 March the dam gave way without warning. Almost a quarter of the central section of the embankment had collapsed, and a wave of water travelling some 30 kilometres per hour swept down the valley towards Sheffield some 11 kilometres away. The valley at Sheffield opened out, and the city was spared a worse fate. Nevertheless parts of it were flooded to a depth of 3 metres, 250 people were killed, and property including homes, factories and mills was destroyed. The Sheffield Union Workhouse with about 1,200 inmates was inundated, but, largely due to the efforts of the matron, Miss Rebecca Day, none of the 'patients' were lost.[9] The official report lists the numbers of horses, cows, donkeys and pigs that were drowned. The disaster naturally had a great effect on the local community, and a broadsheet was published: 'A Copy of Verses Written on the Sad and Awful Calamity that Happened by the Bursting of Bradfield Resevoir [sic] near Sheffield, When Upwards of 240 Human Beings were Swept into Eternity besides a Great Loss of Property':

> Sheffield Town with water to supply,
> They at Bradfield formed a large Reservoir;
> But the bank gave way, and for miles around,
> Men, women, and children have been drowned.

The reasons for the collapse of the dam were never fully explained or understood — thin core wall, loose embankment of wrong material, inadequate overflow, unsupported outlet pipes in the wrong place. The Home Secretary appointed Robert Rawlinson as the government inspector to enquire into the cause of the disaster. Rawlinson was critical of both the design and the construction of the dam. The jury agreed: 'there has not been the engineering skill and that attention to the construction of the works, which their magnitude and importance demanded.'[10] They went on to recommend that there should be legislation to require regular inspection of 'all works of this character'.

There was no Inquiry into the causes, but the water company and the Corporation (who wished to purchase the water company) produced reports whose authors read like a 'Who's Who' of dam engineers of the time. The company engaged Hawksley, Bateman and James Simpson among others, while the Corporation called on nine engineers, including John Rennie, Henry Conybeare, James Leslie and Matthew Jackson. The latter essentially agreed with Rawlinson, and later evidence confirmed the presence of a spring in the cut-off trench which would have had a similar effect to that at Bilberry. As Norman Smith pointed out,

> The Bradfield (Dale Dyke) disaster brought home the fact that the dam-builder has a considerable social responsibility. Well executed, his work is of great benefit to the community, but if it is not, a dam failure is perhaps the most serious man-made catastrophe likely to occur in peacetime.[11]

From the most serious dam failure in Britain, we move to one of the most serious in the world. The dam at South Fork in Johnstown, Pennsylvania, was built in 1838 for that state's Main Line navigation canal and was designed by the state engineer, William E. Morris. It was 22 metres high and had a core of slate, upstream from which was puddle earth covered with loose stone; downstream was rubble masonry with a low-level outlet operated from a tower standing in the reservoir. The dam had a chequered history. No longer used by the canal operators after 1852, it was taken over by anglers; following a blow-out along its outlet in 1862, it was used by the

Pennsylvania Railroad to top up locomotive boilers until it was taken over by a Pittsburgh hunting-and-fishing club around 1880. Fatally, they erected a fish screen above the overflow and raised the dam height by a metre. At the end of May 1889, heavy rain caused the reservoir to fill quickly, overwhelming the spillway and cutting into the embankment, resulting in the collapse of the structure. The water level dropped 20 metres in minutes and 2,209 of the inhabitants of Johnstown were drowned in the ensuing flood.

The power unleashed when a dam bursts is illustrated by what happened to the railway yard. The roundhouse had some nine steam engines in it when the 10-metre-high wave struck. (There were another nineteen or twenty in the yard.) These locomotives, some weighing as much as 80 tons, were scattered anywhere from 100 metres to more than a kilometre from where they had been standing.

So far in this story the dams that failed have generally been of the embankment 'earth' type and the reasons for failure have largely been associated with this construction method – i.e. seepage, overtopping and consequent erosion. Masonry gravity dams presented their own challenges and, as we have seen, towards the middle of the

Site of South Fork Dam, Johnstown, Pennsylvania, c. 1906.

nineteenth century their design began to be associated with theory. It was as the theory was tested by practice that problems occurred.

The Frenchman Maurice Aymard's *Irrigations du Midi de l'Espagne* (1864) was commended to the Algerian Governor-General. This encouraged the French to build a number of irrigation reservoirs in Algeria, the first of which was erected at Habra between 1865 and 1870, so just after the publication of Aymard's book. The Habra masonry dam was designed as a profile of equal resistance but was not well built and was thought to be pervious from the beginning. It was 35 metres high and 325 metres long; in 1881 the inadequate spillway allowed the water level to rise 4 metres above the maximum. The additional pressure is believed to have produced uplift on the water face, and almost a third of the structure failed completely. Tragically, the rebuilt dam collapsed again for the same reason on 26 November 1927.

Another French dam, this time in France itself, at Bouzey near Epinal, collapsed in 1895. Built between 1878 and 1881 to supply the Canal de l'Est, it was 520 metres long and 15 metres high. It was destined to fail, being built on permeable and fissured sandstone; the dam wall had not been carried down to bedrock, and it was poorly constructed and subject to tension on the water face. These factors were the principal causes of the dam's tendency to leak and slide, which happened first in 1884. It was repaired, but again, in 1895, a large part of the wall was destroyed, drowning 150 people. It was noted at the time that, like Habra, the dam at Bouzey was long for its height; this made such structures particularly susceptible to thermal effects. So they would contract in cold weather, opening up vertical cracks – a phenomenon reduced by the curvature in arch dams.

Smith points out that the Bouzey failure is an excellent example of the dictum that more is learned from one unsuccessful structure than from dozens of successful ones. It reminded engineers to build on solid foundations and confirmed the design criteria of Rankine, Augustin de Sazilly and Emile Delocre – it was fatal to allow tensile stresses to develop. It also led to the first theoretical work on uplift pressures in particular – by Maurice Levy in 1895.[12]

Another dam to fail at this time was that at Kesis Gölü in south-eastern Turkey. Built to provide a water supply for the city of Tuspa on the banks of Lake Van, it stored snow melt and then released water as required. The dam was 14 metres high and 76 metres long, but after serving the city for 2,500 years it was destroyed by a flood in 1891. A replacement was built some 50 metres upstream in 1952.

One of the few hydroelectric dams to fail was also one of the first in the US, at Austin, Texas. Like Habra and Bouzey, it was very long (395 metres) relative to its height (20 metres), but it is not known if construction contributed to its failure. It was built on the Colorado River in 1893 and was the first large masonry dam (with a concrete core) constructed for a hydroelectric scheme. On 7 April 1900, heavy rain caused a rapid rise in the Colorado, forming a wall of water over the dam. The dam's downstream toe was eroded, causing the central section to collapse and slide downstream, coming to rest some 10 metres from the rest of the dam. Interestingly, due to siltation, the capacity of the reservoir was only 60 per cent of its original size, which may have restricted its capability to buffer the effects of floodwater.

Austin appears to have been an unfortunate name for a town at the turn of the century in America. In 1901 George C. Bayless started a pulp and paper mill in Austin, Pennsylvania. After a couple of dry autumns it was realized that water storage was required for the mill, and, in 1909, a dam was built on the Freeman Run stream. This concrete gravity dam was 163 metres long and 13 metres high with a central spillway. It was designed by T. Chalkley Hatton of

Delaware with a chief engineer by the name of Rommell. Rommell was noted for reassuring concerned residents that 'the dam will stand when you all are dead.'[13]

In January 1910 a sudden thaw filled the dam to overflowing, and a metre bow appeared on the face of the concrete. People left their homes, but after a week nothing happened and life returned to normal. However, on 30 September 1911, after a month of heavy rain, the dam suddenly blew. The chief of police and Lena Binkey, the chief telephone operator, ran from door to door shouting, 'The dam has broken. Flee to the mountains.' One Madge Nelson had just taken a bath (Saturday was bath day in Austin) when she heard the commotion, looked out of her bedroom window and saw the debris coming down the valley. She did what any frightened girl would have done: 'jumped into bed and covered my head with pillows'. At least 80 people were lost or drowned in the disaster. The broken concrete still stands about 3 kilometres above Main Street, Austin.

It was the failure of a dam for a hydroelectric scheme in Wales

The remains of the concrete gravity dam at Austin, Pennsylvania. The message on the back of the postcard reads: 'Pictures of the Austin Dam 3 mi[les] above Costello in Potter Co. year 1912 Sept. Blanche taught school in Costello. School closed 3 wks. after the dam broke. Abo[u]t 75 killed along the path of the water'.

that nearly led to long-awaited legislation on dam safety in Britain. In 1908, the Aluminium Corporation built the Eigiau Dam at Dolgarrog in North Wales to provide hydroelectricity for the production of aluminium. The concrete structure was further raised to a height of 10 metres with a length of 990 metres in 1911. In 1924 another dam, the Coedty, was built 4 kilometres below Eigiau in order to provide more stored water. This was an earth structure with a central concrete core and of similar height. On 2 November 1925 the clay under the base of the Eigiau was washed away, and, while the dam itself still stood, a gap underneath 22 metres wide and 3 metres deep allowed the reservoir to empty at a rate of a million cubic metres per hour – down the valley and into the Coedty Reservoir. The Coedty Dam, designed to deal with floods from rainfall, was soon overwhelmed, washing away its downstream embankment and causing the core wall to collapse and a breach 60 metres long to release the contents of the reservoir. The water swept down the Conway Valley and flooded the village of Dolgarrog 1.5

Coedty Dam, Dolgarrog, after collapse of 1925.

kilometres below, causing widespread destruction. Fortunately, that Monday evening was the weekly film show in the village hall, so many of the villagers were spared; in all sixteen people drowned.

Patrick Abercrombie, 'the figurehead of rational planning' who played a major role in the planning of Britain's cities after the Second World War, was also a disciple of the Chinese philosophy of feng shui. He believed that the Dolgarrog dams had upset the natural harmony and that 'water . . . resents interference with its natural bent, and as the humble can lose their tempers, it will rage forth from confinement.'[14] However that may be, it was not a good year for the Aluminium Corporation; just ten months earlier, on New Year's Eve 1924, their Cowlyd Dam, built in 1922 in a neighbouring valley and of a similar construction to Coedty, had overflowed, washing away much of its downstream embankment. Happily, the reinforced-concrete core wall remained intact and the dam stood. Also in 1925 a small dam in Scotland failed, discharging the contents of Skelmorlie Reservoir into the Firth of Clyde and drowning several people.

And so at last, some 75 years after the Bilberry inquest had recommended legislation to control dams in the UK, the Reservoirs (Safety Provisions) Act was proposed and passed in 1930. This requires that all reservoirs of greater than 5,000,000-gallon capacity be inspected at least every ten years and that all dams be designed by qualified engineers. Although there has been no major dam disaster involving loss of life since the Act was passed, experience showed that there were weaknesses in the surveillance of dams. This led to the call for an improvement in the legislation, which resulted in the 1975 Reservoirs Act. This was deferred by successive governments (are there really no votes in safety?) and was finally implemented in stages between 1983 and 1987. It introduced improvements to the frequency of safety inspections and made County Councils responsible for enforcement. This resulted in a variable standard of enforcement, and the 2004 Water Bill passed responsibility to the Environment Agency in order to achieve consistency.

In the same fateful decade that led to dam legislation in Britain, the collapse of the St Francis Dam in the US focused minds on safety worldwide. As we have seen, the death toll from the San Francisco earthquake (although the ensuing fire killed many more) and the St Francis Dam collapse was similar; given that the earthquake occurred in a densely populated city while the dam failure affected a sparsely populated rural area, the latter's effect can be seen in perspective.

William Mulholland had built the Los Angeles Aqueduct (LAA) – which passed through the San Francisquito Canyon – from Owens Lake to Los Angeles in 1920. This took water from the farmers and settlers in the Owens Valley (they had been fighting a rearguard action against the Los Angeles Department of Water and Power), culminating in sabotage of the aqueduct. As it entered the San Francisquito Valley a powerhouse was built to capture the hydroelectricity. The plan was then developed to create a reservoir in the valley to power a second plant and to act as a storage/regulating reservoir; this reservoir – the St Francis – would also provide sufficient storage for Los Angeles for a year if anything disastrous happened to the aqueduct.

The valley narrowed to provide a perfect location for an arch dam while the valley was much more open upstream. There was just one problem: the San Francisquito Fault ran through the chosen site. It manifested itself by a junction between conglomerate and mica schist and was known to Mulholland from his earlier times in the area. The concrete arch dam, 60 metres high and 215 metres long, was completed in 1926. As the water level rose in the completed reservoir, it was observed that when it reached the contact between these two rock formations the dam leaked. Attempts to seal it failed, and so a pipe less than a centimetre in diameter was laid on to funnel the leak as a water supply to the home of Tony Harmischfeger, the dam keeper, who lived in a cottage below it.

In the summer of 1927 the LAA *was* blown up — and then threats were received by the department to dynamite the St Francis Dam. However, soon after, several banks in the Owens Valley community failed, and the residents' attention was focused elsewhere. On the morning of 12 March 1928 Mr Harmischfeger called the office in Los Angeles to report an increased flow leaking from the dam. Mulholland was there within two hours, but, finding that the leak was running clear rather than cloudy (which would have indicated erosion of the abutments), he went back to his office for a late lunch. Then at 11.58 p.m., and without warning, the dam broke. A cattle rancher, Chester Smith, sleeping beneath it was woken by the sound of crashing trees and woke his neighbours with that fearful cry, 'The dam has broken.' Death and destruction followed as the wave of water 38 metres high, mud, debris and trees swept to Ventura 87 kilometres down the valley on the Californian coast. There the contents of the St Francis reservoir finally emptied into the Pacific. The precise number of dead and missing is not known, but the Ventura County Coroner's records show 319 and 101 respectively. Commissions of Inquiry and inquests were held, but there was a cloud over the investigations: in April 1928, the Boulder (Hoover) Dam Bill was before Congress. Mulholland maintained throughout the inquiries that the dam had been dynamited by the Owens Valley insurgents, and, if a conspiracy theory needed fuel, a plan to build another reservoir for Los Angeles 700 times as large as St Francis would be it. The true cause of the collapse will probably never be known, but it is likely that poor foundations where the wings met poor rock formations were contributory factors. Whatever the cause, Mulholland told the Los Angeles Coroner, 'If there is an error of human judgement, I was the human.'[15] Mulholland retired from the Los Angeles Department of Water and Power later that year at the age of 73 after a distinguished career of more than 50 years, more than 26 of those as Chief Engineer and General Manager. He spent the rest of his life as a recluse and died in 1935.

Mulholland's story is fictionalized in the 1974 Roman Polanski film *Chinatown*, which has 'Hollis Mulwray' as the city water commissioner who refuses to build a new dam following the collapse of his earlier efforts. He is murdered for his obstinacy. While loosely based on facts, this story is maintained by commentators to have perpetuated the theory that 'metropolitan interests illegally and immorally appropriated the Owens Valley for their own expansionary purposes.' It is perhaps no coincidence that, soon after the film's release, explosions destroyed spill gates on the aqueduct. In 1978 an arrow tied with dynamite struck and damaged William Mulholland's statue in Los Angeles.[16]

Such was the fear raised by the collapse of the St Francis Dam that it was thought that others built by Mulholland would fail. The Mulholland Dam above Hollywood, completed in 1925, impounded Lake Hollywood and was emptied by 25 per cent for safety reasons and quietly renamed 'Hollywood Dam'. The Hollywood Dam 'endures as an exquisite creation, an example of municipal Mission-style architecture'. Mulholland said at the opening ceremony, 'I wanted something ornamental and architectural as well as useful. The structure is itself the best tribute.'[17] Ironically, in the 1974 film *Earthquake* (dir. Mark Robson), the Hollywood Dam *does* indeed break, flooding the town and fulfilling the fears prophesied by the producer David Horsley, who had filed a lawsuit in 1928 against the Los Angeles Water Department, believing that the lives of 250,000 people were threatened by a dam 'doomed to failure – built by the same men with the same materials (as St Francis)'.[18]

With improved standards and inspections, the safety records of dams worldwide improved, and for more than 30 years there were few notable collapses in peacetime. On 2 December 1959 another arch dam – this time in France – collapsed. The unfortunately named Malpasset (sounding like, 'goes badly'), 66 metres high, was a concrete arch dam south west of Nice. It failed as it was being filled for the first time, killing 421 people, more than 300 of whom were in the town of Fréjus. The design was by André Coyne, who was experimenting with thin-arch dams – one at Tolla in Corsica was only a maximum of 2.5 metres thick – in effect running full-scale trials. As Norman Smith said, however successful such thin dams are, they may not be psychologically justifiable.[19] The subsequent inquiry into the cause of the Malpasset failure found there to be 'weakness in the foundation rock – a finding which in itself gave an incentive to the study of rock mechanics'. This tragedy marred the end of Coyne's career, and he died the following year at the age of 68.

The Mulholland Dam, California, renamed Hollywood after the collapse of the designer's dam at St Francis.

The greatest dam disaster in Europe in recent years occurred without the dam collapsing. The most ambitious dam designed by the Italian engineer Carlo Semenza was the Vaiont hydropower dam, built in 1960 in a narrow gorge 95 kilometres north of Venice. This variable-radius concrete dam was one of the world's tallest at the time at 262 metres high but was only 190 metres long. After heavy rains in 1963, the rising water caused a massive rock slide which filled the reservoir, resulting in a huge wave 60 metres high that overtopped the dam and drowned more than 2,500 people. The dam itself was virtually unscathed.

In the US, the worst dam disaster since the war occurred in 1976 on the Teton River in Idaho. Against considerable local opposition an earth-fill embankment dam was built by the US Bureau of Reclamation for flood control and irrigation. It was 90 metres high and 950 metres long. Construction began in February 1972; it was topped out in November 1975 and it began to fill. By May 1976 water depth had reached 56 metres. A heavy snow in the winter of 1975/6 began to thaw, and, although the reservoir was designed to fill at less than half a metre per day, permission was granted to fill it three times as fast.

Inspection teams on the morning of 5 June noticed some seepages and at 9.10 a.m. muddy water (a sure sign of erosion) was seen coming from the face: 'At about 10.30 a.m., a loud roar and the sound of rapidly running water were heard.'[20] Two bulldozers were sent to begin pushing rock into the eroding hole. At 11.30 they fell into it; fortunately, their drivers had jumped clear. One third of the embankment crest had collapsed by 11.55. An area of 775 square kilometres was flooded. Remarkably 'only' eleven people were lost although 25,000 were left homeless; damage was estimated at $400,000,000. The investigating panel concluded that the failure was due to seepage through cracks in the fill material and between that material and the rock formation. The death toll was believed to be so low due to the prompt warning and evacuation procedure. In 1986 the Bureau announced that it was ready to rebuild the dam. Not surprisingly the communities of the Teton Valley declined the offer. As we saw earlier, tailings dams are potentially the most dangerous. In 1985 at Trento in North East Italy, the tailings dam for a fluorite mine collapsed releasing a tide of 200,000 cubic metres of toxic waste to flow at 90 km/hour down the Stava Valley. Two hundred and sixty-eight people were drowned in addition to the destruction and subsequent contamination. Poor construction and maintenance were to blame.

A far greater disaster due to dam failure occurred in 1975 in Henan Province in China. Although there was a news blackout at the time (to this day the Chinese authorities prefer to manage the media during emergencies), some details emerged subsequently. China has always been plagued by floods. In the Huai River basin, weather systems from north-central Asia meet those from the South China Sea – the result is regular flooding, which the government of the PRC decided to address in 1950, calling their programme 'Harness the Huai River'. Two major dams were built – the Banqiao and the Shimantan. They were followed by many smaller dams, first in the mountains and then on the plains. One of China's foremost hydrologists, Chen Xing, was involved in the design of these dams; he criticized this policy and was purged as a 'right-wing opportunist'. He had advocated twelve sluice gates on the Banqiao but was accused of being too conservative, and the number was reduced to five.

In August 1975 a typhoon hit Henan Province. The rainstorm lasted for three days and the reservoirs quickly filled to capacity: water could not be released fast enough by the reduced number of sluices. Both dams collapsed at about midnight on 8 August. A wave 10 kilometres wide and 7 metres high rushed down the valley. There was no time for warnings. It is not known how many people were lost – some reports say 85,000, but many died from the resulting epidemics and famine as well as from drowning, putting the total figure nearer to 150,000. Several dams were deliberately destroyed by the air force to release water in desired directions. After the disaster, Chen Xing was brought back to advise on clearing the river channels. In all, more than 3,000 dams were destroyed as a result of the typhoon.

As we saw earlier, tailings dams are potentially the most dangerous. In 1985 at Trento in North East Italy, the tailings dam for a fluorite mine collapsed releasing a tide of 200,000 cubic metres of toxic waste to flow at 90 km/hour down the Stava Valley. Two hundred and sixty-eight people were drowned in addition to the destruction and subsequent contamination. Poor construction and maintenance were to blame.

A scheme that was eventually built in 1993 despite opposition and that suffered a rare failure (rare for the UK) was Carsington. This scheme had been designed for Severn Trent Water Authority to improve supplies to the East Midlands, to Derby, Nottingham and Leicester. It received approval in 1978 after three public inquiries in 1971, 1973 and 1977. Construction began in 1980, but failure of the dam during embanking occurred in 1984 and after careful investigation the scheme was redesigned by Babtie, Shaw and Morton. It covers 300 hectares and provides river regulation of the Trent for abstraction on the Derwent. Its initial failure led to the trend for an independent design panel to review major dam design and construction in Britain.

With passing years, the best dam sites are adopted and less than perfect locations have to be considered: rock mechanics can help to evaluate such options. However, it is not always possible to avoid inherently dangerous areas such as earthquake zones – for example in Iran, India, and Japan – and it is necessary to include allowance for the effects of seismic activity in design calculations.

Really large reservoirs can actually *cause* earthquakes. Lake Kariba, between Zambia and Zimbabwe, contains 170,000 metric tons of water and produced two earth tremors soon after it was filled. Lake Mead, behind the Hoover Dam, contains 37 billion tons of water and caused an 18cm depression in the Earth's surface when filled for the first time. The most serious case of damage, however, was at Koyna Dam in India in 1967. This dam is 104 metres high and contains 2,800 million cubic metres of water. Seismic activity started as it was being filled, causing an earthquake that was measurable throughout the world and that resulted in 200 deaths in the city of Koynanagar south of Mumbai.

Dams have also been used to cause disasters. The 3-metre-high wall of the Mantinea Dam, built in around 1000 BC and used by the Myceneans for storage of rain and snow melt in the Peloponnese, was deliberately breached in 418 BC during the Peloponnesian War. This was the first known act of war against a dam. Some thousand years later, the Chinese adopted the tactic of *shnigong* (literally, 'against by water'). This took the form of either building or breaching dams in order to flood enemy positions. The most spectacular was used in AD 514 on the River Huai near Fushan. A remarkable 32-metre-high, 4-kilometre-long embankment dam was built to flood an enemy position upstream. Unfortunately, only four months later the river overtopped the dam, and the breach drowned 10,000 people downstream: the dam turned itself on its makers.

During the Spanish conquest of the Aztecs, dams and dykes built in 1440 in Lake Texcoco were fiercely fought over. General Franco continued the tradition during the Spanish Civil War when his troops unsuccessfully attempted to blow up the Ordunte Dam near Bilbao. During the Second World War, there were German plans to destroy the Aswan Dam, and in 1941, as we have seen, the retreating Russian army blew up the Dnieprostroi Dam even though their

own people were escaping across it at the time.

Dam disasters make great film themes. *Dam on the Yellow River* (Renzo Merusi, 1960) tells the allegedly true story of a 1949 Communist plot to blow up a dam 'to convince the world of our power'. In the film, rafts full of explosives are floated to the dam. The hero (played by George Marshall) reaches one of the rafts but is too late, and the dam blows up, costing 'millions of lives'.

The reason many British people are aware of dams was due to the RAF attacks on the German ones on the Ruhr in 1943. As early as 1937, dams supplying water and power to the industrial heartland of the Ruhr were seen as Germany's Achilles' heel. Various experiments were tried and failed, including one by Barnes Neville Wallis of Vickers Armstrong at Weybridge in Surrey to drop a 10-ton bomb on a dam. Since no aircraft existed to carry such a payload, he designed a six-engine bomber, but it was then realized that it would

This one is dynamite! Publicity for *The Dam on the Yellow River*.

need a 1000-metre runway to take off so the plan was abandoned. Scale experiments on the Nant y Gro half-completed dam in the Elan Valley proved that explosives actually had to be in contact with a dam's wall to be effective, so Barnes Wallis decided to develop a missile that could reach a dam in a series of ricochets with back spin such that it would crawl down the dam on contact rather than bounce off. Following a successful experiment against the luckless Nant y Gro in September 1942, Sir Henry Tizard, scientific advisor to the Air Ministry, asked Barnes Wallis 'to submit an opinion as to whether a "bouncing bomb" could be fitted to a . . . Lancaster'[21] bomber. A number of British dams and reservoirs were used to test the theory. First Barnes Wallis flew over Queen Mary Reservoir in south-west London to test the effect on aircraft of carrying spinning bombs. Then, during tests off Chesil Beach on the Dorset coast in January 1943, he succeeded in enticing his 'bombs' to bounce – first once, then thirteen and finally twenty times – sufficient to cover the length of water to reach a target. Following this success, he reported that seven dams should be targeted: the Möhne, Sorpe, Lister, Ennepe and Henne, which held water that supplied the domestic and industrial needs of the Ruhr, and the Eder and Diemel in the Weser Valley further east. The latter fed the 320-kilometre Mittelland Canal linking the Rhine with Berlin. Air Chief Marshal Arthur 'Bomber' Harris called the plans 'tripe of the wildest description' but was overruled by Chief of Air Staff A.C.M. Portal, who gave the instruction to proceed. This was at the end of February 1943, and the attack had to be mounted before the end of May, after which the water in the reservoirs would begin to be drawn down, leaving them too shallow for the 'bombs' to be effective. This did not leave much time to design a real 'bomb', assemble and train the air crews, and acquire and adapt twenty Lancaster bombers.

Despite 'Bomber' Harris's initial reluctance, he nominated Acting

Wing-Commander Guy Penrose Gibson to assemble 617 Squadron based at Scampton in Lincolnshire, and it was not long before Gibson was flying over Derwent Reservoir trailing a 45-metre length of chain to practise the required flying height. Meanwhile Wallis developed his 'bomb' (which was really a 4,500-kilogram mine), discarding an original barrel shape clad in wood for a 1.5-metre steel cylinder some 1.2 metres in diameter. With six days before the target date of 19 May 1943 the 'bomb' eventually bounced in trials in the sea off Reculver in Kent. Different reservoirs were used for training: the Eyebrook Reservoir in Rutland, which supplied Corby steelworks, represented the Möhne Dam (with the addition of canvas sheets to simulate the towers); the Abberton Reservoir near Colchester represented the Eder Dam; and the Howden and Derwent represented the Sorpe.

When the operation order was signed on 15 May, the Henne Dam was omitted since it was considered to have too much anti-aircraft

A Lancaster bomber in 1986 recreating a Dambuster training flight over the 1912 masonry Derwent Dam.

protection. So the main targets were the arch gravity dams of Möhne, Lister, Ennepe, Eder and Diemel and the embankment dam with concrete core of Sorpe. The first wave of bombers on the night of 16 May attacked the Möhne. When news reached Scampton that it was breached at the third attempt, Harris told Wallis that although

The Möhne Dam in the Ruhr before and after the Dambusters' raid in May 1943.

A Dambusters' raid print signed by 'Johnny' Johnson, bomb aimer on the attack on the Sorpe Dam.

he had been sceptical at first 'you could sell me a pink elephant now.' Factories, power stations and houses up to 65 kilometres away were either destroyed or damaged in the Ruhr valleys, and more than 1,300 people were dead or missing. The Eder was also breached and power stations were destroyed, but, owing to better warning and a flatter valley, only 47 people died. The attack on the Sorpe was more conventional in that the 'bombs' were dropped on to the dam, but despite two direct hits it suffered only minor damage. The Ennepe was attacked but not damaged.

Out of nineteen aircraft that flew to Germany that night, eight did not return. The effects on morale for Britain and its allies probably counted for more than the damage – the dams were all repaired by October. However, the reservoirs were kept deliberately low afterwards, and power and agricultural produce were reduced for months, at a time when they were most needed. The claim in the *Illustrated London News* that 'RAF Smash Europe's Mightiest Dams' may be an exaggeration, but 617 Squadron deserved its newly adopted motto, '*Aprés moi le deluge.*' It may have been the last fighting unit to have such a commendation, since under the 1972 Geneva Convention attacks on dams are banned. Whether the successors of eco-warrior George Washington Hayduke in Edward Abbey's 'The Monkey Wrench Gang'[22] will abide by such conventions is another matter: in 1981 they unfurled a plastic 'gash' on the concrete wall of Glen Canyon Dam on the Colorado River, upstream from the Grand Canyon.

In the construction of dams, accidents do happen and lives have been lost as a result of challenging working conditions. However, a natural disaster that probably could not have been foreseen occurred in Switzerland in 1965. The dam at Mattmark was under construction when an ice avalanche from a glacier hit the labour camp on 30 August. Eighty-eight workers were killed.

Dams *do* have to be maintained, of course, as the effects of Hurricane Katrina testified in 2005. Much of New Orleans lies below sea level and is protected by a system of canals with concrete walls to keep the water out of the city. Katrina caused these walls to fail, leaving 80 per cent of the city flooded, thousands dead or injured, half a million people displaced and $100 billion of damage. The exact cause is still disputed, but it is now accepted that it was a failure in the system rather than the inadequate height of the levees. There are questions about whether there really was a system, in fact, but if there was it had been developed in a piecemeal fashion, with inconsistent levels of protection.[23] The water levels were actually below the levels of the walls, and the floodwater seeped through the underlying weak foundations, thus undermining the structures. At 17th Street Canal, the levee was breached when the concrete walls tilted, causing a 60-metre length of the barrier to break away. However, there are reports that the responsible body, the US Corps of Engineers, knew about these weaknesses from reports prepared as long ago as the 1980s and took no remedial action.[24] While climate change is resulting in no more hurricanes per season, they are becoming wetter and more powerful, so repair and maintenance is becoming a matter of urgency for the Corps of Engineers. In their defence it has to be said that they were not the ones who built a major settlement on a swamp in the first place.

While this chapter has recounted numerous failures, when viewed against a total of 45,000 large dams worldwide, the overall picture must be one of success. Those dams that have failed by accident have essentially been 'accidents waiting to happen', due either to poor design or to poor construction. Even when an embankment dam is hit with two 45,000-kilogram bombs it still stands, a testimony to the soundness of the theory that has at last caught up with practice.

5 | Dam Angry

I'm agin Dams!
Ella Garth in *Wild River* (dir. Elia Kazan), 1960

Many hundreds of thousands of dams have been built throughout the world, yet it is only in the past hundred years or so that resistance to their construction has manifested itself. This has coincided with an increased appreciation of our environment through the writings of the Romantic poets and the philosophical pronouncements of John Ruskin and his followers; a growth in the organization of environmental concerns; and a need to build dams in more sensitive or populous regions to meet the needs of the burgeoning world population. Organizations, notably the International Rivers Network and the World Wildlife Fund (WWF) have set themselves the task of closely monitoring dam projects and rallying opposition, while ICOLD is seen as aligning itself with dam proponents.

Early (isolated) opposition occurred in Britain in the nineteenth century in response to proposals to develop England's Lake District for the water supply of Liverpool and Manchester. In 1874 J. F. La Trobe Bateman proposed that these two cities undertake a joint venture to exploit Ullswater as a source of supply. However, in 1877 it was proposed that Liverpool could independently develop the valley of the Vyrnwy in North Wales, a view endorsed by George Deacon, the Liverpool Borough Engineer. While the members of the Water Committee preferred a joint scheme, it was apparent that their

opposite numbers in Manchester were not so enthusiastic, and, as we have seen, Vyrnwy was pursued by Liverpool.

Bateman now suggested that Manchester should go it alone and develop Thirlmere, a glacial lake originally divided by a bridge. It was proposed to raise Thirlmere's level by some 15 metres and to construct an aqueduct 160 kilometres long to Manchester. The gathering ground was some 4,000 hectares at the head of 'the romantic Vale of St John's'.[1] When the residents of the then counties of Cumberland and Westmorland heard of the proposals, a Thirlmere Defence Association was formed, supported by 'lovers of nature, beauty and heritage from throughout the English speaking world'.[2] These included such luminaries as John Ruskin, Thomas Carlyle and Matthew Arnold together with Octavia Hill and Robert

Postcard of Thirlmere in the Lake District, looking south from the 1890s dam.

Hunter (who founded the National Trust in 1894). The Association maintained that 'It is almost a trite remark that the one mountain region in England is in a very high sense the property of all Englishmen. To the nation it is a gift coming direct from the hand of God.'[3] This organized opposition managed to forestall the proposals until 1879, when the Thirlmere Water Bill was approved by Parliament. Construction did not start until 1890 due to trade depression and reduced demand for water, but when Manchester Corporation did decide to proceed they appointed Bateman's pupil George Henry Hill as the engineer. The gravity dam itself is only 20 metres high but with foundations 17 metres below the toe; it is constructed of rock 'plums' embedded in concrete, with a masonry face.

There were two significant features of the Thirlmere scheme. First the resistance was not just mounted by local property interests. Newspaper reports at the time claimed that 'the lake country belongs in a sense and that the widest and best sense, not to a few owners of mountain pasture but to the people of England.[4] So this was a foretaste of what was to come in the twentieth century (and was followed soon after by the campaign to save Hetch Hetchy in California). The Corporation claimed, in terms that have since become familiar to opponents of reservoir schemes, 'that the works will enhance the natural beauties in the district'; equally familiar nowadays, the emotional wish from Ruskin was that 'Manchester would drown in the water it wanted to steal.' Thirlmere was also important since it heralded the 'Manchester conditions' implemented by the subsequent Haweswater scheme. These provided that any district within 5 miles of the aqueduct should be granted bulk supply of water at cost – effectively buying off much opposition.

Meanwhile in California, John Muir, probably the first conservationist to take up a pen against dams, was exploring the Yosemite east of San Francisco. Born on 2 April 1838 in Dunbar, Scotland,

Muir was the son of a grain merchant who decided to emigrate to America in 1849 in the cause of his religious freedom. On their Fountain Lake Farm in Wisconsin, the younger Muir made model sawmills and waterwheels and dammed brooks until, at the age of 22, he finally left to make his way in the world. After a spell at the University of Wisconsin, he discovered botany and hiked for weeks into Canada, where he worked with his brother in a sawmill. It did not occur to him then that this mill could literally eat up the forests he found so beautiful.

Muir arrived in San Francisco in 1868 via Florida and Cuba. Inspired by a brochure of the hotelier John Mason Hutchings, he became a shepherd in Yosemite. Although he travelled widely, Yosemite was his spiritual home from then on. It was made a national park in 1890, two years before Muir and his friends formed the Sierra Club to preserve the Sierra Nevada forests and mountains. (Today the Sierra Club has more than 1 million members worldwide). In the spring of 1902 President Theodore Roosevelt, just six months into his presidency, joined Muir camping and hiking in Yosemite on a fact-finding mission regarding the management and exploitation of forests.

In 1903 James Phelan, then Mayor of San Francisco, applied to Congress for permission to dam the Tuolumne River and form a reservoir in the Hetch Hetchy Valley in the north of the park for a water supply for San Francisco. The application was turned down not once but three times by Roosevelt's Secretary of the Interior, E. A. Hitchcock – until the earthquake of 1906. In the days that followed it, Phelan attempted to make political capital out of the disaster by claiming that there would have been plenty of water if his applications had been approved. The truth was that there *was* plenty of water; the water mains had fractured in the quake.

In September 1907 the Sierra Club sent a resolution to Congress formally objecting to the damming of Hetch Hetchy: 'Since there are other adequate sources of water available for San Francisco, it is only just to the nation at large, which is vitally interested in preserving the wonders of Yosemite National Park, that their destruction . . . should be avoided . . . '[5] Note the striking similarity between this approach – claiming that the environment belongs to the nation, not just to local interests – and that adopted by the Thirlmere Defence Association. The project's promoters claimed that damming Hetch Hetchy would enhance its beauty by forming a crystal-clear lake. To this Muir retorted as follows:

> Landscape gardens, places of recreation and worship, are never made beautiful by destroying and burying them . . . these temple destroyers seem to have a perfect contempt for Nature and instead of lifting their eyes to the God of the Mountains, lift them to the Almighty Dollar.[6]

In 1908 the newly appointed Secretary for the Interior, James R. Garfield, approved the fourth application, subject to San Francisco not finding suitable sources of water elsewhere. The Sierra Club and its supporters wrote hundreds of letters to Congressmen and anyone who could exercise some influence, especially the Federation of Women's Clubs. In March 1909 William Taft assumed the presidency and replaced Garfield with Richard Achilles Ballinger. With dissenters within the Sierra Club, the opponents of the Hetch Hetchy scheme formed a separate 'Society for Preservation of National Parks, California Branch', with John Muir as their President. He wrote, 'Dam Hetch Hetchy! As well dam for water-tanks the people's cathedrals and churches, for no holier temple has ever been consecrated by the heart of man.'[7]

In September 1909, Muir, now over 70, was companion to his second US President in Yosemite when he guided President

William Taft along the trails there. Consequently Ballinger asked the dam promoters to show why Hetch Hetchy should not be removed from the permission granted by his predecessor. This hearing in May 1910 was the first of many postponements in which San Francisco was given more time to 'show cause'.

In the summer of 1911 Muir told his friends that he was about to fulfil a lifelong dream and visit the Amazon; to spare their concern he neglected to tell them that he was also going to Central Africa. So he saw Victoria Falls and the source of the Nile, returning to America via the Red Sea and Mediterranean.

With a new President, Woodrow Wilson, in the White House in 1913, the dam promoters lost little time in influencing Congress. Pamphlets were distributed illustrated with pictures of Swiss lakes to show how fine it would be to change Hetch Hetchy from a meadow to a reservoir. The Raker Bill to give permission for the dam was heard by a House Committee in July and brought to the floor of the House in September, when many Congressmen were away. The Bill was passed by 183 to 43 with 205 absent. The Senate passed it in December 1913, and Wilson signed it a few weeks later. Muir died a year later – of pneumonia (not of a broken heart, as many commentators have suggested).

The O'Shaughnessy Dam was started in 1915 and completed in 1922. It is named after the San Francisco City Engineer, Michael Maurice O'Shaughnessy (also the engineer for the Golden Gate Bridge) and is a curved gravity concrete dam. Originally 69 metres tall, in 1938 it was raised in height (as had been planned by its designers) by 26 metres, increasing the area at top water level of the reservoir from 643 to 798 hectares. In 1962–4 the Canyon Power Tunnel was completed to increase the power output of hydroelectricity.

Opposition did not go away, however, and activists aping the Monkey Wrench Gang painted a vertical crack on the dam face in the 1980s. In a surprise announcement in 1987, the then Secretary of the Interior, Donald Hodel, proposed to remove the dam and restore the valley. The Sierra Club reasserted its original opposition, and the Bureau of Reclamation agreed that 'such restoration would renew the national commitment to . . . keep in perpetual conservation an irreplaceable and unique natural area'.[8] Whether or not the deconstruction ever takes place, the words of the landscape architect Frederick Law Olmsted, who was appointed by the State of California in 1864 to prepare a management plan for Yosemite State Park, may well be decisive: 'structures should not detract from the dignity of the scene.'[9]

Opposition to dams was usually localized in the early years of big dam-building – riparian owners, competing cities (London and Birmingham, for example) and strangely, in the US, between rival developers (the Corps of Engineers and the Bureau of Reclamation were often at odds in developing competing schemes). Things came to a head in Montana and the Dakotas in the 1940s, but, predictably enough, these agencies were not the losers.

The Bureau had a plan before Congress for the development for irrigation of the Upper Missouri in Montana while the Corps had their plan for five big dams on 1250 km of the Missouri in North and South Dakota. The two schemes were irreconcilable, and President Franklin Roosevelt proposed to break the stalemate by creating a 'TVA' for the Missouri basin. This was not in either agency's interest, so they quickly developed a joint plan which actually amounted to an adoption of both of their original ones.

The Native American Three Tribes (Mandan, Hidatsa and Arikara) lived on the Fort Berthold Reservation, some of the best and most fertile bottom land on the Missouri. At the time, the reservation was approximately 1,200,000 hectares (having been reduced from the 4,800,000 hectares granted under the Fort

Laramie Treaty of 1851). Flooding as a result of the proposed 64-metre-high, 4-kilometre-long Garrison Dam would reduce this land to less than 400,000 hectares. Interestingly, no 'white' towns would be affected by any of the Corps reservoirs – in fact the height of Garrison was to be reduced by 6 metres to ensure that the town of Williston, North Dakota, remained dry.

The Three Tribes pleaded with the government to reject the plan, saying that 'the homes and lands of 349 families – 1544 individuals will be covered.'[10] However, when the Department of the Interior decided to support the plan, the Three Tribes resorted to negotiation. They asked for compensatory land, electricity, grazing and watering rights for their cattle and a bridge across the narrowest point of the reservoir so that occupants of the reservation could stay in touch with one another.

During the negotiations, a dissident group from the Three Tribes, led by Thomas Spotted Wolf, dressed for the warpath, burst into the room and hurled insults at Brig.-Gen. Lewis A. Pick of the Corps, who was a no-nonsense military man. Pick exacted his revenge through friends in Congress, and the draft agreement was torn up and a new one prepared by him was adopted. According to it the tribes were not to fish in the reservoir, their cattle could not graze its margins nor drink from its waters, there were to be no rights to electricity, and compensation moneys could not be used to hire attorneys. The chairman of the Fort Berthold Indian Tribe Council, George Gillette, said when agreeing to the sale of the tribes' best land: 'The members of the Tribal Council sign the contract with heavy hearts . . . Right now the future does not look good to us.'[11] The white landowners saw the value of their property rise by 3,000 percent, and a motel – 'The Best Motel by a Damsite' – opened for business in 1946. As a final insult the Corps named the reservoir Lake Sakakawea after the interpreter who had

INDIAN CHIEF THOMAS SPOTTED WOLF LEVELS HIS FINGER AT ARMY OFFICERS, SHOUTS, "YOU HAVE COME TO DESTROY US!"

accompanied the first white explorers in the region. The Three Tribes finally had to settle for compensation of $33 per acre lost — out of which they had to pay for relocation and reconstruction of their villages.

The Garrison Dam is one of the largest earth-rolled dams in the world. Construction began in 1946 and was complete by 1954 and generating power by 1956. The Corps today claim that the waters of the lake provide a variety of benefits including recreation and irrigation. The Three Tribes' way of life was almost completely destroyed by Garrison Dam: they had lived in the area for a thou-

'You have come to destroy us': Native American Chief Thomas Spotted Wolf accuses Brigadier-General Lewis A. Pick of the US Corps of Engineers, 1946.

sand years (thus developing a sense of history the Corps could not comprehend) and lost 94 per cent of their agricultural lands. Farms were liquidated, unemployment reached 70 per cent, and the community life so essential to their culture was lost. It was to take a generation before the tribes showed signs of recovery.

In the UK at this time, the British Electricity Authority (BEA) was developing an ambitious plan for maximum development of hydroelectric power principally to be concentrated, due to topography, in Scotland and Wales. The Welsh Nationalists took particular exception to this on the grounds that it was their water and that the grand schemes would benefit English industry while the Welsh in their remote farmsteads would no doubt still have to rely on generators. In Amabel and Clough Williams-Ellis's *Headlong Down the Years*, a polemic against the schemes, Mr Galvanic, the public-relations agent for the BEA, exclaims 'If I had my way, this disgusting water would soon know its place! The place for water is behind dams and in pipes − all under control.' The Welsh Bard

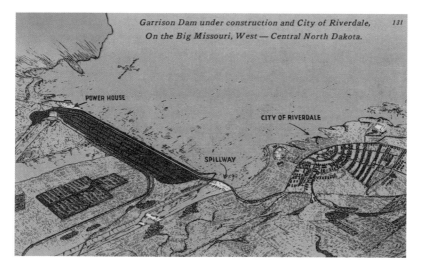

Garrison Dam, Montana, as planned.

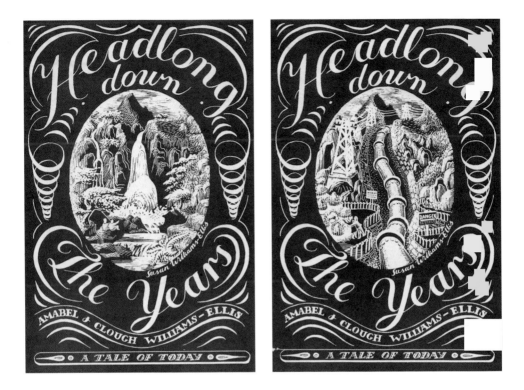

rejoined, 'We have defended ourselves and our mountains for centuries! You will never tame our earth . . . or our rivers!'[12]

Consequently, the North Wales Hydro Electric Power Act of 1952 included an Amenity Clause for schemes in Snowdonia requiring the appointment of a landscape architect to preserve amenity and scenery for such schemes. This clause was inserted largely at the behest of the Council for the Protection of Rural Wales, of which Clough Williams-Ellis was President, and marked a turning point in the recognition of environmental issues raised by dams in Britain. It also extended the composition of the design team from being solely engineers.

Before and after: the jacket of *Headlong Down the Years: A Tale of Today* by Amabel and Clough Williams-Ellis, 1951.

The National Parks and Access to the Countryside Act was passed in 1949, fulfilling a long-standing environmental commitment by the Labour Party. This established the Nature Conservancy, whose main role was to create a series of protected sites such as National Nature Reserves and Sites of Special Scientific Interest (SSSI). In 1950 the Conservancy designated an area in the Pennines in north-east England known as Cow Green where an unusual set of geological conditions provided the habitat for rare alpine plants known as the Teesdale Assemblage.

In 1956 the Tees Valley Water Board promoted a scheme to meet the requirements of chemical (principally for ICI) and engineering works on Teeside. The proposed site was upstream from Cauldron Snout, a waterfall much visited by tourists since Victorian times, where the River Tees cascades over the igneous rocks that intrude into the surrounding limestone. The Conservancy objected to the potential loss of habitat only to be described by Water Board members as 'cranks'. This confrontational approach led to one of the most protracted and antagonistic debates about a proposed reservoir in the UK. Having initially considered the Cow Green site in 1956 and encountered considerable opposition, the Water Board decided to promote an alternative impounding reservoir at Balderhead on the River Balder. This was completed in 1964 just as ICI advised the Water Board that, due to the planned introduction of two new ammonia plants, additional water was required. Sandeman, Kennard and Partners were instructed by the Board to investigate source options and, once again, Cow Green was favoured.

Roy Gregory maintained in *The Politics of Physical Resources* that it was important to the Water Board and ICI that 'the reservoir should not provoke serious opposition'.[13] However, given the earlier controversy, seeking to promote a reservoir in an SSSI could not have been seen as a trouble-free proposal. However, a meeting was

'High Force or Fall of Tees', downstream of the proposed Cow Green Dam; an 1850 engraving by J. Landseer after J.M.W. Turner.

Cow Green Dam: half the dam to the left is embankment, while the dam to the right is concrete gravity.

held between Julius Kennard, the design engineer, and Max Nicholson, the Director General of the Conservancy, from which Kennard formed the impression that Cow Green was not the most objectionable of the possible alternative sites.[14] After a second meeting, Nicholson (who had consulted with his regional officers and received letters opposing the scheme from the Botanical Society of the British Isles [BSBI] as well as from a young David Bellamy), wrote to Kennard that 'it was most unlikely that the Cow Green site would be objected to . . . indeed the Conservancy might feel justified in actively supporting such a project in face of opposition from certain quarters.'[15] (In the examination before the House of Commons Select Committee in May 1966, Kennard said he thought 'we had achieved a remarkable victory,' to which his QC replied, 'you achieved a remarkable letter.')[16]

Soon after these meetings, Alderman Allison, chairman of the Water Board, announced the proposals for a reservoir at Cow Green. David Bellamy pleaded via an article in the *Northern Echo* 'that everything should be done to keep the reservoir out of this great biologically important area.'[17] From now on much of the debate was conducted through the press and not always in the politest of terms. Alderman Allison asked whether 'people who think more of flowers . . . than of industry can impose their will?'[18] A plethora of objections continued to arrive at the Durham County Planning Office with both the Council for the Protection of Rural England and the Society for the Promotion of Nature Reserves adding their voices to the campaign. In July 1965 the Conservancy advised the Water Board that it intended to object to Cow Green, but indicated that it would be prepared to discuss an alternative site in the Moor House National Nature Reserve upstream from Cow Green to avoid injury to features of high scientific interest. As Max Nicholson (clearly having been shown the error of his ways!), stated to the press, 'the objection is to the dam site, not the reservoir . . . the Conservancy regard the problem as a model of how conflicting interests of conservation and science could be resolved.'[19]

In view of Alderman Allison's response, this may have been premature. As he put it, 'we examined the territory on Friday and never saw one flower. The Labour Government made a grave mistake when they gave the Nature Conservancy unlimited powers.'[20] (The Alpine type flowers tend to flower in the spring; Allison and colleagues visited in August.) At the opening of the Balderhead Reservoir in October 1965, Allison had told Richard Crossman (then Minister for Housing and Local Government) that Cow Green was needed to provide for the future. While Crossman recorded his visit to open Balderhead, 'the largest earth-dam in Great Britain',[21] in his diaries, he made no mention of this conversation, though he perhaps had cause to remember it later.

The Bill promoting Cow Green was laid before Parliament on 27 November 1965. Just before Christmas, a meeting was held between the Water Board and their consulting engineers and officers of the various County and Rural District Councils concerned. The meeting was advised that Frederick Gibberd had been retained 'to landscape the Cow Green development'.[22] Westmorland County Council wanted consultations on landscaping and requested a 'Manchester clause' to be inserted.

The Bill received its First Reading to the House of Commons in January 1966 and was referred to a Select Committee for detailed consideration in May. During the intervening period there was considerable debate, discussion and correspondence on amendments as well as vigorous lobbying to influence Members of Parliament. Crossman recorded in his diaries that 'while there are serious objections on the ground that rare mosses . . . will be destroyed . . . the case was objectively difficult to defend but I got it through [Cabinet] in twenty minutes.'[23] Not only had Crossman listened to Alderman Allison, but the government had decided on the outcome of the debate.

Gibberd, in his evidence to the Select Committee, agreed under cross-examination that he would regard the dam as 'an arrogant artificial structure . . . if I were not designing it'.[24] His phraseology in this instance could certainly be regarded as 'arrogant'. In the event, he did not influence the dam design or its location, and it is not possible to conclude what his opinion of the final design actually was.

The Bill was approved on a free vote in the Commons and returned to the Lords for its Second Reading. Having lost the battle in the Commons, where members were bound to be influenced by the employment issues in their constituencies, the Teesdale Defence Committee felt they could win by emphasizing general landscape and amenity issues rather than just the scientific uniqueness of Upper Teesdale.[25] The Bill received this reading but was sent on to a Select Committee with a Special Instruction that consideration should be given to other sites for reservoirs. Gibberd gave evidence to this Committee that 'the dam . . . would be a rather splendid sight and no disfigurement of the environment need take place at all.'[26]

On 23 January 1967, fourteen months after the Bill had first been laid before Parliament, the Committee recommended approval to the Lords, noting that alternative schemes would cost in the region of £9,000,000 compared to the £2–2,500,000 for Cow Green. Cow Green was eventually constructed in 1970 with the Cauldron Snout waterfall protected, but not all observers consider that the resulting dam sits comfortably in the landscape. David Bellamy described it as a 'white elephant'.[27] The dam is unusual, being partly earth embankment and partly concrete gravity to take account of the varying geology. It is accepted that earth mounding in front of the concrete could have mitigated its starkness, but Alderman Allison had won his victory and was in no mood for compromise.

This again, then, like Thirlmere and Hetch Hetchy, was a scheme that had been opposed on national-interest grounds, making full use of increasing national environmental legislation. The development of the European Union Environmental Directives gave opposition groups an added international armoury, but not even this had any effect in Cardiff Bay. With the decline of the steel industry and the docks, the idea of forming a barrage across the bay to create a freshwater lake was conceived by the Secretary of State for Wales in 1986. The Cardiff Bay Development Corporation was formed with the aim of creating prime development land from the dereliction – all surrounding a 'Fake Lake', as Friends of the Earth called it. However, not only was the Severn Estuary (of which Cardiff Bay is a part) an SSSI; it was also a Special Protection Area in accordance with the European Birds Directive – and a Ramsar wetland site of international importance, being home to thousands of over-wintering wildfowl.

Apart from the RSPB, others formed the Cardiff Residents Against the Barrage. Because the barrage would also block a navigable waterway, it needed its own Act of Parliament. From 1987, six Bills were presented for parliamentary scrutiny. The last was supported by an Environmental Statement in accordance with the European Directive on Environmental Impact Assessment. Eventually, in 1993, the Cardiff Bay Barrage Act was passed, and by 2001 a muddy estuary of 160 hectares of Tiger Bay had been turned into a freshwater lake at a cost of £200,000,000. It costs £20,000,000 a year to run to keep the groundwater from rising, to oxygenate, filter and dredge the lake, and to operate the floodgates. A further £10,000,000 were spent creating mudflats and salt marsh for the evicted waders and wildfowl on 300 hectares of the Gwent Levels. The 1.1 km barrage has, however, resulted in a £2 billion regeneration of the old dock areas.

One of the most controversial of dam projects, and certainly the longest running, is the Narmada Valley Development Project in India. The Narmada flows for more than 1,300 kilometres through the states of Madhya Pradesh, Gujarat and Maharashtra to the Arabian Sea. Plans for harnessing the river for irrigation and power generation were conceived as early as 1946 by the British. The riparian states could not agree on the relative share of water and power, and in 1964 the government appointed a committee, which recommended a 183-metre-high dam at Sardar Sarovar. Still no agreement could be reached, and the Narmada Water Disputes Tribunal was

The 'Fake Lake' of Cardiff Bay, from the front cover of a brochure for the Cardiff Bay barrage.

established in 1969, giving its final award decision in 1979. This proposed the construction of nearly 3,200 structures of which 30 would be major dams; a 450-kilometre canal would transfer some water to Rajasthan. The terminal dam at Sardar Sarovar, the only one in Gujarat, is a 1,210-metre-long concrete gravity dam.

Apart from irrigation of drought-prone areas and power generation, the project was intended to provide drinking water and flood protection principally for Gujarat. Some 20,000,000 people live in the valley, and 1,000,000 needed to be resettled as part of the scheme. These 'oustees', as they are called, were provided for by the approval notice. There was to be a loss of 500 square kilometres of teak and hardwood forest, for which compensatory re-forestation was proposed. In 1985 the World Bank sanctioned credit for the project and was instrumental in securing the best resettlement programme India had ever proposed. Indeed, there was no conception in India up to that time that oustees should be rehabilitated and resettled. However, the World Bank withdrew its support in 1993,

Sardar Sarovar Dam on the Narmada River, Gujarat.

principally on the basis (ironically enough) of the inadequacy of resettlement proposals.

Protests against the dam had started in 1989, when 60,000 tribal groups, environmentalists and peace activists had gathered in Madhya Pradesh, providing a focus for the Indian environmental movement. This generated international interest and further independent reviews of the project. Accordingly, in 1994 the construction of the dam at Sardar Sarovar was challenged in the courts by the Narmada Bhachao Andolan (NBA – Save Narmada Campaign). After six years, the Supreme Court ruled that construction should continue, allowing the dam height to rise to 90 metres. Every 5-metre increase thereafter would be subject to environmental clearance by the government up to the full height, which is now planned to be 138 metres.

The international profile of the Sardar Sarovar project has no doubt been raised by the involvement of the 1997 Booker Prize winner, Arundhati Roy. In 1999 Roy wrote *The Cost of Living* – a treatise against big dams – which the Delhi Supreme Court saw as an affront to its dignity, and she led a march to villages which were to be drowned that year by the rising reservoir waters. She was eventually accused of inciting violence and of contempt for demonstrating against the court's decision to go ahead with the dam. This adverse publicity has cooled the interest of major Western contractors.

The major problem with the scheme has been that the promised proposals for resettlement of the oustee farmers and fishermen have not been implemented. Madhya Pradesh has declared that it does not have the land on which to settle the people from the Narmada Valley. As Roy said, 'while the judges are discussing our contempt of court, people will stand chest deep in water for days; thousands of cases for compensation for lost land are pending [and yet] the bench will spend days discussing my case.'[28] The State of Gujarat, on the other hand, protests that all this is misinformation spread by an 'internationally sponsored anti-dam campaign with local counterparts'. They take the view that if it is all right for the West to have dammed its rivers then why shouldn't developing countries do likewise?[29] The furore over the Narmada proposals was instrumental in securing the investigation of the World Commission on Dams. At the consultation session, a representative from NBA made the point that 'if you can't resettle, you have no right to displace.'[30]

The usefulness of having an internationally recognized personality supporting the cause was demonstrated in Tasmania in 1983, with a more successful outcome (so far). In 1978 the Tasmanian Hydro Electric Commission announced its intention of building the Franklin Dam on the Gordon River in south-west Tasmania. The plans polarized the Tasmanian community with, initially, 70 per cent in favour – believing that the dam would bring jobs and industry to a poor area.

However, a protest movement soon gathered momentum. A campaign was co-ordinated by the Tasmanian Wilderness Society, the Tasmanian Conservation Trust and the Australian Conservation Foundation. Within two weeks, 30,000 letters of protest were generated and a film, *The Last Wild River*, was shown on Tasmanian television.

In 1980, 10,000 people marched on the State parliament in Hobart, and the Labour State government offered to re-site the dam upstream to reduce the area of wilderness destroyed. This met with little approval, with the anti-dam groups opposing any dams in the region. The Liberal State Legislative Council blocked the compromise anyway, insisting that the original proposal be implemented.

In 1981, Don Clipp, an Australian Senator, initiated an inquiry into 'the natural values of southwest Tasmania to Australia and the world' – i.e., pursuing the 'this is more than local' Thirlmere argument. As might be expected there was a flurry of studies – Aboriginal caves with hand stencils and stone tools up to 24,000 years old were found.

At the end of 1981 a State referendum was held to try to break the deadlock. However, there were only two options: keep to the original site or choose a compromise one. Forty-five per cent of voters spoiled their papers. The crisis led to the overthrow of the Labour government and the election of a pro-dam Liberal Party, which immediately ordered the original plan to be built and threatened to secede from the Commonwealth if the federal government interfered.

The anti-dam campaigners blockaded the site on 14 December 1982 when UNESCO was to announce that the Tasmanian rivers were to be listed as a World Heritage Site. Twenty-five hundred people came from all over Tasmania and overseas to the river – with an equal number attending a rally in Hobart in favour of the dam. The construction site turned into a daily battleground, with 1,200 people being arrested for impeding the works. Five hundred were jailed for breaking the terms of their bail, including the British botanist David Bellamy, who had cut his campaigning teeth on the Cow Green Reservoir some twenty years before.

A rally, this time attracting 20,000, was held in Hobart in February 1983, and a flotilla of boats took to the Gordon River in March; a full-page advert appeared in Australian newspapers asking, 'Could you vote for a party that would destroy this?' It did the job. On 5 March the Labour Party, led by Bob Hawke, who had committed to stop the dam, won the federal election. The new government passed the World Heritage Properties Conservation Act, giving it powers to override state legislation. On 1 July 1983 the High Court voted 4:3 in favour of the federal government. The dam plans were shelved, and no further hydroelectric dams have been proposed in Australia since then.

Decisions affecting dam projects influenced by outsiders are epitomized by the projected Chalillo Dam in Belize. Belize (former British Honduras) is a member of the Commonwealth and borders the Caribbean in Central America. The government proposed a 35-metre-high, 360-metre-long concrete gravity dam on the Macal River in the Maya Mountains in Southern Belize. The reservoir would flood 11 square kilometres of the valley, including 800 hectares of rainforest, home to 36 rare or threatened species such as the scarlet macaw and the jaguar. A Canadian company won the contract to build and operate the dam, securing exclusive water rights to the river as well as the sole rights to sell electricity to the people of Belize.

The Belize Alliance of Conservation Non-Governmental Organizations (BACONGO) was formed to oppose the project. BACONGO, supported by Princess Anne, Harrison Ford and Cameron Diaz, filed two civil law suits in 2002 against the dam, on the basis that due process was not followed and questioning the adequacy of the environmental assessment. The dam's promoter thinks the project has been hijacked by environmental terrorists; the objectors view it as an environmental crime. The Belize Court of Appeal refused to grant an injunction, and so BACONGO appealed to the Privy Council in London, being the final court of appeal for Commonwealth countries. While refusing to grant an injunction, the Privy Council did eventually hear the appeal but ruled in January 2004 that the dam could go ahead. A strange tale indeed: a British court rules that a Canadian company can build a dam in a third country.

Politics plays a major role in dam-building; indeed it has been said that there is an 'Iron Triangle' between politicians (who need to be seen to be doing something), dam promoters (who are in the business of providing dams) and contractors (who want to build them). This triangle is demonstrated by the controversial hydro-electric Pergau Dam in Malaysia near to the border with Thailand. In 1988, Britain signed a defence export protocol with Malaysia such that the country would receive 20 per cent of any arms contracts in the form of aid – the Aid and Trade Provision (ATP).

Six weeks after the signing of the protocol, an application for aid through the ATP for the Pergau Dam was made to the UK's Department of Trade and Industry (DTI). Assistance was offered but withdrawn in 1990 when the DTI concluded that Malaysian consumers could purchase electricity more cheaply from gas-turbine power stations. So, although one half of the British government was opposed to the granting of aid, the Ministry of Defence lobbied Prime Minister Margaret Thatcher on the effect on arms sales. The offer of £200,000,000 was confirmed, and in 1991 building of the dam began – at the same time as Malaysia bought £1 billion worth of arms from Britain. A judicial review was heard by the High Court in 1994, when the link between arms and aid was ruled illegal. Ironically, the Malaysian government was so upset by this implied association with 'sleaze' that it banned further awards of contracts to British firms! The earth-embankment dam was completed in 1997 – 67 metres high and 750 metres long.

Another controversial project that was reliant on British aid is the Ilisu Dam in eastern Turkey. This dam is on the headwaters of the Tigris and, if implemented, would reduce the flow to Syria and Iraq, affecting water supplies and the livelihoods of farmers. Just as critically, it would flood the Kurdish homeland, including the medieval town of Hasankeyf, designated as being of archaeological importance in 1978 by the Turkish government. An Ilisu Dam Campaign was mounted to stop British involvement in the dam, and this was successful. In 2000, MPs rejected the proposed support for the scheme on the basis of human-rights contravention as well as the

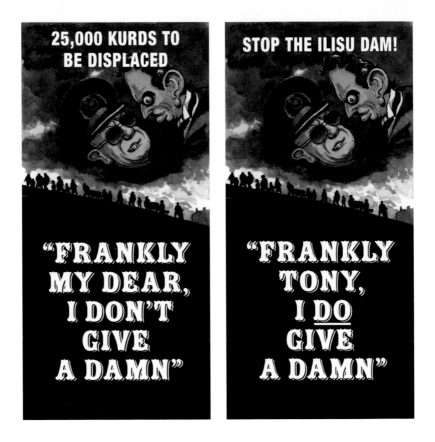

potential for cross-border tension. Eventually, the British contractor (the same one building the Pergau) pulled out of the project.

The dam, 65 kilometres north of the Syrian and Iraq borders, is proposed as 135 metres high and 1,820 metres long. It was first proposed in 1954, but lack of financing prevented rapid development, and it was not until 1982 that the design was approved. There was conflict between Turkish security forces and the Kurds at this time, and the World Bank and other funding agencies were unwilling to finance such a controversial scheme. In 2005 the scheme was resurrected – this time to be built by a German contractor but with new resettlement plans for the 70,000 displaced Kurds and measures to

Ilisu Dam, Turkey: cartoons opposing the scheme, based on a sketch by Steve Bell.

'rescue' parts of Hasankeyf. The saga continues – in 2007, a Swiss bank funding the scheme withdrew its support.

Resettlement issues also figured in the Victoria Dam in Sri Lanka, completed in 1984. It flooded more than a hundred villages, affecting 50,000 people, with resettled families each receiving £90 compensation. Families who owned their own houses were given the market value – although this only applied to a few. They were also offered 1 hectare of land – usually forest which had to be cleared, thus adding to the overall environmental impact. In terms of the oustees displaced and potential power generation, IUCN reported Victoria Dam as displacing 214 people per MW. This does not compare favourably with the Itaipu, for example, which only displaced 5 per MW. The dam itself, 120 metres high and with a crest of 520 metres, is unique among the dams of Sri Lanka in being of a double-curvature (cupola) arch design with radial gate spillways set at the apex of the arch.

Victoria Dam cupola concrete dam completed in 1984 in Sri Lanka.

The Victoria Dam on the Mahaweli Ganga is only one part of the Mahaweli Development Project initiated in the 1950s to bring land under cultivation, provide irrigation and generate electricity. Unfortunately, agricultural land is in short supply in Sri Lanka, and there was opposition on the grounds that valuable valley land would be lost — as well as the traditional tank water management system practised for thousands of years. The scheme comprises five reservoirs as well as trans-basin diversions and connections and now provides over 50 per cent of national electricity production. Although a beautiful dam type, the reservoir has not been at capacity for some 20 years since the power company take much of the stored water for power generation. Representations were made to the World Commission on Dams inquiry in 1999 to permanently reduce the water level in order to bring agricultural land back into use and to rectify the poor compensation. The Commission was (somewhat hopefully) also asked to consider recommending the decommissioning of the whole project and replacing it with a series of run-of-the-river power stations. To their credit, further projects by the Mahaweli Authority have retained the traditional systems.

One of the most extraordinary projects that was actually supported by the American environmental movement — including the Sierra Club founded by John Muir — was the Glen Canyon Dam on the Arizona–Utah border. It arose out of the Bureau of Reclamation's grand plan — the Colorado River Storage Project — to regulate and control the whole catchment. The first proposal in 1955 was to build a dam at Echo Park on the Green River in Utah, which would have flooded the Dinosaur National Monument. David Brower, as Director of the Sierra Club (which had lost at Hetch Hetchy), was determined to win this time round. A publicity campaign was mounted generating thousands of letters to Congress. After a protracted battle, Echo Park was abandoned in 1956 — but at a price. Dams would be built at Flaming Gorge (in 1964) and at Glen Canyon (completed in 1963). Glen Canyon is the tallest (at 213 metres) concrete arch dam in the US and created Lake Powell (named, some might say cynically, after the explorer of the Colorado, John Wesley Powell), a 115-km-long reservoir.

Brower had actually proposed building Glen Canyon to an even greater height, providing more storage and thus saving Echo Park. Later, however, as he rowed down the Colorado when the dam was being built, he realized what he had done. So he mounted a last-ditch effort to save the canyon. The 'no-compromise' Floyd Dominy declared that the reservoir would enable people to see the walls better from boats. In response, Brower ran an advertisement in the *New York Times* asking, 'should we also flood the Sistine Chapel so tourists can get nearer the ceiling?' The dam was opened in 1966 by Lady Bird Johnson, and Brower and Dominy took a boat trip together on the lake. Dominy claimed that he was the bigger environmentalist: 'I've changed the environment, yes, but I've changed it for the benefit of man!'[31] Brower was ousted from the Sierra Club in 1965 as a result of a disagreement over financial management; he went off and formed the more radical Friends of the Earth. In 1995 he was back on the Sierra Club board, and in 1996 he persuaded them to support a proposal to drain Lake Powell. With the reservoir silting up fast and evaporation and seepage taking their toll, the day may indeed come when this happens.

Dam removal is now the clarion cry of the environmental movement, and dam owners and operators fear this scenario – once one was drained it would be harder to defend the rest.[32] In 2002, President George W. Bush set up the Klamath River Basin Working Group to look at issues in the catchment area in Oregon to improve water quality and quantity. It recommended removal of the Chiloquin Dam on the Sprague River; the agreement to implement

this recommendation was signed in 2006. In 2004 members of four Native American tribes had besieged Scottish Power's AGM in Edinburgh claiming that a subsidiary, PacifiCorp, had damaged salmon stocks and their livelihood with its dams on the Klamath River. They wanted the 53-metre-tall Iron Gate Dam, built in 1962, removed and fish ladders installed so that the salmon could move more easily along the river. However, although the dams were originally planned to provide energy, upstream farmers depend on irrigation water diverted from the Klamath. Scottish Power said they had not ruled anything out or in. They subsequently sold PacifiCorp.

Dam removal continues in the US, but, while 185 have been removed since 1999, they were mostly small dams that had reached the end of their working life. As the American Rivers Unplugged

Glen Canyon Dam, Arizona.

Campaign has said, 'There comes a time in the life of many dams when they begin to make less sense than they did in the past.'[33] Dam removal is not to be undertaken lightly, however, since the sudden discharge of sediment built up over many years can bring problems of its own.

From dams unsuccessfully opposed by conservationists to the coming of age of the environmental movement, the abandonment of dam projects as a result of pressure, and proposals for the removal of dams, the wheel has turned full circle. Mont Saint-Michel, the island between Normandy and Brittany on the north-west coast of France, was inscribed on the UNESCO World Heritage list in 1979. In the 1880s, Victor Hugo had written, 'Mont St Michel must remain an island.' In 2003 permission was obtained by conservationists to *erect* a dam to achieve just that. The island's character had changed since Hugo's time: in 1879 a causeway had been built for pilgrims, and a dam on the River Conesnon had been created in the 1960s to protect agricultural land upstream. These actions had restrained the daily scouring effects of tide and river, and gradually salt marsh was strangling the Mount. The plan now being implemented includes a new dam to manage the currents to generate a flushing action to clear the build-up of the sediment. Sluices will release water on the ebb tide to clear the sand from around the Mount – expected to take some ten years from construction. Such a scheme has of course not been without controversy – the 60 Montois (as the residents of the Mount are known) wonder how they are to reach their homes via a 2-kilometre pedestrian bridge from the mainland. They are also concerned for the 3,000,000 tourists who visit the Mount every year and the income they generate. However, if Mont Saint-Michel ceased to be an island, its allure would surely diminish.

For Marc Reisner, the twentieth century was the 'Hydraulic Century, the Age of Dams'. He felt that 'there never was . . . an era of such gargantuan and disruptive civil engineering works.'[34] Reisner did not live to see the publication of the World Commission on Dams report, so his reaction to its findings can only be imagined. In 2005 the WWF produced a report, *Dam Right – To Dam or Not to Dam?*, a review of the five years since the WCD published their findings.[35] They recognized that rising fuel prices and energy demands, as well as worldwide commitments to the Kyoto Protocol to arrest climate change, had resulted in a renewed focus on developing hydropower. They looked in particular at dams which had been approved since the WCD report.

One of the WCD's case studies has been the Mekong River basin, where, over the last ten years, more than a hundred dams have been proposed. The Mekong rises in the Himalayas in Tibet and flows for 4,800 kilometres through China, Burma, Thailand, Cambodia and Laos before reaching the South China Sea south of Ho Chi Minh City in Vietnam. According to the International Rivers Network (IRN) more than 60,000,000 people depend on the Mekong for food, water and transport. In an ideal world, development of such a resource would follow an integrated river-basin management plan for mutual benefit, but, with so many interested parties, this is a forlorn hope. China has plans for eight dams on the Upper Mekong with two completed and a further three under construction; this is in accordance with the Western Development plan to supply energy to the eastern cities of Beijing, Shanghai and Guangdong. China has half of the world's 45,000 dams, and, while the Three Gorges Project has attracted much controversy, other schemes have proceeded largely unnoticed. While these projects provide energy and clean water for people in China, they change the lives of millions downstream. The natural flood/drought cycle and transport of sediment affects the natural ecosystem as well as the livelihoods of the populations of much of south-east Asia; already fisheries and water levels are changing.

In Thailand, a campaign has been mounted to decommission two dams built in the 1990s. At Pak Mun Dam, 5,000 villagers occupied the site in 1999 and refused to leave until the gates of the dam were permanently opened. They achieved a short-lived victory in 2001 when the Thai government opened the gates, but it closed them again in 2002. In Vietnam, which built 500 dams in the 40 years to 1999, the government halted progress on the Son La Dam while plans were prepared for the resettlement of 100,000 people.

The WWF took as a case study the Nam Theun 2 (NT2) Dam project, which has been under consideration since the 1980s when the hydropower potential of the Theun was first realized. Laos has a low population density and poor infrastructure, and the United Nations Development Programme saw hydropower as a major factor in economic growth, offering an opportunity for revenue from neighbouring countries. The NT2 will be a gravity dam 39 metres high and will create a reservoir of 450 square kilometres. This will require the resettlement of 6,000 villagers and will affect between 50,000 and 100,000 people who depend on the fisheries in the catchment for their livelihood. Following WCD principles, an environmental and social programme has been initiated together with extensive community consultation. The World Bank and the Asian Development Bank (ADB), which approved funding for the project in 2005, are closely monitoring it to ensure that construction is synchronized with a relocation programme and environmental management. The World Bank maintains that Thailand has agreed to purchase the electricity generated, and Laos is committed to the standards laid down by the Bank – which will reduce its lending if Laos does not comply.[36] On a 2006 visit the IRN found that fisheries were already being affected by construction; there was a lack of compensation for loss of crops and inadequate baseline surveys and monitoring – clearly 'not perfect but could be worse'. Of greatest concern is the fact that, as a precondition of World Bank support, the Lao government enacted a National Policy on Environmental and Social Sustainability of the hydropower sector and this is not being implemented. The consequence is that there is no environmental impact assessment or social-development plan for the hydro-schemes under construction. This is a flagrant breach of the World Bank precondition and could result in termination of the funding, which would jeopardize the efforts which the government has made for resettlement of villagers.

The WWF takes the view that, while accepting that Laos needs sustainable economic development, the economic, social and environmental risks of the scheme are considerable. As a measure of whether the WCD principles are being met, the WWF is not reassured that the Strategic Priority for Comprehensive Options Assessment – especially in terms of need and alternatives – has been met. The WWF think that there is a case for moving back from a project-by-project approach and adopting a basin-wide view, taking into account the cumulative impacts of these multiple dams on one catchment.

However, while finding much to criticize with continuing projects throughout the world, there are signs, in the eyes of the WWF, of encouragement. In 2004 even China temporarily halted the Three Gorges Project to set up the Yangtze Forum to improve both the relationships with those affected by the scheme and the environmental management of the river. The WCD recommendations are now used as a reference point for funding institutions. With due consideration and the skills of engineers, the days of reservoirs on the Indus silting up within a generation or of dams being built in Africa with no consideration for diseases such as malaria or bilharzia will hopefully be behind us. Perhaps peace may finally break out in the world of dams. How engineers have faced such social and environmental issues is the subject of the final chapter, where we will see that conflict is not always necessary.

6 What Environment?

The benefits and impacts of dams have become one of the battle-grounds of the sustainable development arena.
— Nelson Mandela

We have seen that dams and their reservoirs have, from the earliest times of human development, provided for the sustainability of humankind. They have protected communities from flooding, provided power, drinking water and water for irrigation, and facilitated navigation. In so doing they have created 'new' environments for wildlife, recreation and amenity. Some have extolled their virtues in this respect.[1] But what of protection of an existing valued environment, be it natural, heritage or landscape? And what of the communities threatened by loss of their towns, villages and land?

In the US the first national park was established in Yellowstone in 1872, but there was no real system of such parks until the National Parks Service was created in 1916. Similarly, protection of the environment emerged in the latter half of the nineteenth century in the UK by such measures as the Alkali Acts (1863) to reduce air pollution and the Rivers Pollution Prevention Act 1876. It generally took a calamity to force protection on to the statute book, including the cholera outbreak in London in the 1830s and '40s and the 'Great Stink', which resulted in legislation for sewage treatment. The London smog of 1952, which resulted in thousands of deaths, led to the Clean Air Acts of 1956.

The post-war Labour Government in Britain was committed to protection of the *natural* environment and introduced the National Parks and Access to the Countryside Act 1949, which recognized landscape and wildlife value by means of Areas of Outstanding Natural Beauty, SSSIs, national parks and nature reserves. It also set up the necessary administrative bodies to undertake research, designation and management of such areas: the Nature Conservancy and the Countryside Commission. By this Act, it became an offence to develop or undertake prohibited operations in such designated areas. The Act therefore played a significant role in the battle for Cow Green, as we have seen. Such legislation was replicated to a greater or lesser extent worldwide, but in many instances enforcement was hamstrung by lack of resources and/or manpower.

A significant step forward came 20 years later with the adoption of the National Environmental Protection Act in the US. This required an Environmental Impact Assessment (EIA) for infrastructure or industrial-development proposals above a given magnitude. In summary, EIA allows for the assessment of potential impacts on the environment and their significance, as well as measures proposed to mitigate such impacts.

The practice of EIA was rapidly adopted by governments throughout the world and by the European Union in 1985. Significantly, it was also adopted by funding agencies such as the World Bank as a check alongside the social and economic viability of proposed major developments. In 1996, the Bank reviewed the performance and impacts of 50 of its funded schemes. Others, such as ICOLD in 1997, produced guidance for proponents of dam projects. Other pressures for environmental protection have arisen from the adoption of policies for sustainable development at the United Nations Conference on Environment and Development (UNCED) at Rio de Janiero in 1992.

However, these movements, policies, guidance and legislation have not been the panacea that was hoped for. Indeed, the conflicts surrounding dam proposals continued to escalate, so the World Commission on Dams was set up in 1998 to investigate and review experience of dam development and make recommendations for planning in the future.[2] The Commission was established at a conference at Gland in Switzerland hosted by the World Bank and the International Union for the Conservation of Nature. It concluded its work in 2000 with the launch of its report in London (which is where Nelson Mandela pronounced that 'The benefits and impacts of dams have become one of the battlegrounds of the sustainable development arena'). The strategic priorities set by the Commission are: gaining public acceptance; comprehensive options assessment; addressing existing dams; sustaining rivers and livelihoods; recognizing entitlements and sharing benefits; ensuring compliance; and sharing rivers for peace, development and security. They require that dam promoters screen out projects that are inappropriate and that their advisers should ensure that schemes are socially and environmentally acceptable.

The influences and pressures on design engineers to increase the degree of mitigation in designs have been referred to as the 'Design Squeeze'.[3] Such pressures include the approval process, legislation, pressure groups and safety considerations, as well as the composition of design teams. But did it just take legislation, threats and Commissions to cajole engineers into considering the environment when proposing new dams? Was there evidence that engineers had always thought of the potential effects of their actions when considering locations, scale and extent of reservoirs, and the new landscapes they would create or the losses that would ensue? The short answer is probably 'Not a lot', but as always there are exceptions which prove the rule.

Britain was at the forefront of the Industrial Revolution, and, while numerous dams for mill power had been created since the beginning of the nineteenth century, the burgeoning population drawn to the major metropolises placed new demands on water supply. In particular, Birmingham in the Midlands, unusually not sited on a major river, drew on shallow wells for its supply. With population growth and sewage and industrial discharges, the groundwater began to be of doubtful quality. As we have seen, the Elan Valley scheme was promoted to alleviate the problem. The engineer, James Mansergh, had proposed compensation water of 22.5 million gallons per day (mgd), but the rod fishermen on the River Wye claimed a requirement of 40 mgd: the Parliamentary Committee ultimately approved 27 mgd. Apart from compensation water, most of the objections were on the basis of compulsory purchase and loss of fishing, shooting, pasture, mineral rights, fisheries and spawning grounds. This latter objection was described as 'a sportsman's petition promoted in the interests of a few rich fishermen who object to even the remotest possible interference with their amusements'.[4] As Mansergh stated, 'there is practically no salmon fishing on the Elan and very little if any spawning ground upon the Elan and the Claerwen above the Caban . . . it is a sport rather than food of other people at 1/3d per pound – eating salmon is a luxury and fishing with a rod an occupation for the rich.'[5]

Writing in 1907 in a guide book to Rhayader and the highlands and lakes of mid-Wales, L. H. Evans and R. Darlington extolled the virtues and beauty of the new reservoirs 'that from their size, the intricacy of their wanderings amid rocky scenery of beauty and grandeur, deserved to be classed as lakes'. While these 'unsullied, cloud-enriched valleys were, on the advice of James Mansergh and others, determined as the site of the reservoirs',[6] the authors appear to have been suitably impressed by the care that has been taken to help nature back to her own whenever it would add to the beauty and comeliness of the scene; we find the unique pleasure of combining the beauty of nature with the triumph of human ingenuity, labour and skill set side by side in such a way as to cure the despondency of the overworked brain to assure it once more that it is a good world to live in, where nature is so fair and man so triumphant in his energy and skill.[7]

Sylvia Crowe, writing about the Claerwen Dam (completed in 1952), was concerned about the 'appurtenances' that of necessity accompany dams. A total of three public car parks had been provided, and she demonstrated ways of concealing them and restoring the balance of the view when it could 'become a magnificent composition in civil engineering'.[8] Crowe was rather scathing regarding the decision to leave an island in the new lake of Pen-y-Gareg – 'an incongruous blob of black [which] obstructs the view of the dam'[9] planted with conifers. It has to be remembered, however, that Mansergh was working before the formation of the National Trust in 1894 and more than 50 years before any hint of legislative consideration of environmental issues. We may accord him some credit.

The same could not be said of London. Having opposed Birmingham at the Parliamentary Committee stage (and lost) because the metropolis judged it might want Welsh water for itself, it opted for river abstraction and storage in bank-side reservoirs along the Thames to the west of the city. Built at the same time as Elan, they were designed with a standard uniform cross-section and were regular in plan to a varying geometric shape. This despite being within view of Windsor Castle and close to Runnymede, where the Magna Carta was signed (as Barbara Carroll has pointed out, itself an early recipe for sustainability).[10] No concessions were offered to this historic setting, and they remain to this day – easy enough to maintain and inspect but inhospitable and forbidding from the outside. However, as we have noted, these same reservoirs provide safe places for wildfowl to rest and feed during their vulnerable moulting period, and they have been designated SSSIs since 1975 and as a Special Protection Area in accordance with the EU Directive on the Conservation of Wild Birds in 2000. Nevertheless, Crowe saw these reservoirs (and their cousins in the Lea Valley to the east of London) as 'more of a liability than an asset to the landscape'.[11] Tom Turner described the bunds as 'resembling railway embankments'.[12]

Another city feeling the pressure of inadequate water supplies in the 1930s was Bristol. From the mid-nineteenth century it had obtained its water from springs in the Mendip Hills some 40 kilometres to the south of the city. (The aqueduct or 'line of works' for transfer of the water to local storage reservoirs where it was treated had an air valve some 15 metres tall which was disguised as an obelisk in 1850 – an early example of mitigation of visual impact.)

The City Engineer identified a natural basin in the Chew Valley 15 kilometres south of Bristol for a new reservoir. It was determined that an embankment 365 metres long and just 13 metres high could create a 485-hectare reservoir with a capacity of 20 million cubic metres. Accordingly a Bill was presented to Parliament in 1939. The Bill was opposed by, among others, the local authorities and riparian owners, principally to protect their interests and ensure adequate provision of compensation water. However, Axbridge Rural District Council, as the planning authority, were also concerned about the injurious effects on the amenities, natural interest and beauty of the area. Although a relatively sparsely populated place, a total of seventeen cottages and nine farms would be lost by the scheme, with a hundred people to be rehoused. Royal Assent was granted in July 1939, and the Bristol Waterworks Act of 1939 authorized the Bristol Waterworks Company to acquire land by compulsory purchase. However, despite the loss of this valuable agricultural tract, all lands were acquired by private negotiation.

The outbreak of war delayed the start of construction, and when, in 1945, water consumption began rising again, Ministry approval for funding was sought. However, due to capital expenditure restrictions at this time it was not until 1950 that approval was given.

The loss of the fertile valley with its traditional farmsteads, manors and mills was viewed with concern by some and with resigned equanimity by others: the greatest concern was to record features and buildings before they were lost. In this respect it was fortunate that the Bristol Waterworks official F. C. Jones was also an antiquarian and local historian. He realized the area's potential hidden treasures, and every support was provided by the Company by means of excavation facilities. The Ancient Monuments Department of the Ministry of Works had been interested in the effects of the scheme since 1949, when it had become apparent that a number of historic buildings would be lost. These included Walley Court, a medieval and Queen Anne building near to the proposed embankment; Spring Farm, with a magnificent tithe barn; and Stratford Mill, an eighteenth-century corn mill which was dismantled and rebuilt at Blaise Castle Estate in Bristol. In 1953, the Ministry of Works, knowing that the valley had been inhabited from the Neolithic period, decided to embark on a systematic archaeological investigation prior to flooding. This revealed evidence of settlements from the Bronze Age, Iron Age and Roman period, including graves and numerous artefacts: the most significant find was a Roman wooden writing tablet with an ink inscription, which had survived immersion in water for 1,600 years.

The clearance works involved the loss of a hundred kilometres of hedgerows and more than 3,000 mature trees. The reservoir works involved the diversion of roads and the provision of new carriageways on embankments at various locations – at the southernmost edge of the new lake at Herriotts Bridge this formed 8.5 hectares of very shallow water. The engineers decided that since 'this would form an unsightly area when the water level dropped, it was decided to "pond up" this expanse permanently'.[13] This area has now become a nature reserve managed by the Avon Wildlife Trust. Conversely, at Herons Green to the west, the road embankment was made watertight to protect valuable farmland.

The Company realized that, given the reservoir's location near Bristol, it would soon become a visitor attraction, and they appear to have been concerned at the outset to ensure that the site was managed accordingly. The amenity value was paramount, and while fishing was encouraged it was not until 1967 that sailing was permitted. The Company's policy was 'not merely to preserve the existing amenity but wherever possible to enhance it'.[14]

In this respect the Company may have been encouraged by a clause in the Bristol Waterworks Act of 1917, for the construction of their Cheddar Reservoir which required it to take 'all reasonable regard to the preservation of the beauty of the scenery of the district'. The design and materials used for the various structures received special consideration, and many trees and shrubs were planted – the architect Kenneth Nealon was retained to design various staff cottages as well as Woodford Lodge for anglers. While landscape architects had been required by Act of Parliament to be appointed to hydroelectric schemes in Wales by 1952, no landscape specialist was engaged on Chew Valley. However, it was the first reservoir to be designed incorporating recreational facilities.[15] Queen Elizabeth II commented at the opening ceremony on 17 April 1956 on the tree planting to heal the (inevitable) scars, the opportunities for wildlife and the provision of a pleasant place for recreation. The report of the Queen's visit noted that the Company 'had aimed to make this a piece of lakeland scenery pleasing to see rather than simply a utilitarian reservoir'.[16] The commercial value of the hundreds of thousands of trees initially planted as amenity planting was of secondary importance. The amenity of the reservoir was greatly improved by Denny Island, a high point in the valley on which trees were planted in advance of the flooding in 1952. However, an additional artificial island was abandoned when the Ministry declined to fund the £18,000 cost. Fishing was encouraged; the lake was stocked with more than 200,000 trout and facilities were provided for anglers. The fish were provided solely as an amenity – the 'Company felt that as it had the privilege of controlling various large and suitable expanses of water it had a duty to provide good fishing'.

Apart from being scenically attractive and a mecca for angling, bird-watching and sailing, the lake was designated as a SSSI in 1972 and, later, as a Special Protection Area for birds under the EC Birds Directive. This occurred because of the lake's size and its attractive position for migrating and wintering birds. The flooding of this lowland valley meant that natural and gently shelving banks with extensive shallows supporting a rich marginal vegetation were formed.

While Bristol Waterworks reservoirs have always considered amenity (Blagdon Lake was stocked with trout in 1904), particular care was taken at Chew, both in its initial design and in its later operation and management. In this respect the 1966 Circular on the Use of Reservoirs and Gathering Grounds for Recreation by the Ministry of Land and Natural Resources, to promote easier public access to reservoirs, led to a great increase in recreational use. All this occurred at Chew before there was a statutory requirement to do so. While Bristol Waterworks had bought some of the farms, 'there was surprisingly little protest and little evidence of [protest] from parish council minutes . . . they just took it for granted'.[17]

With such glimmers of promise for environmental protection prior to legislative encouragement, it may have been expected that numerous examples of sites rejected for environmental reasons could be cited. Unfortunately for the environment, such examples are few and far between, and they were abandoned due to public outcry and opposition rather than the choice of engineers.

It is still seen as the engineer's duty to find the most suitable site with maximum capacity at least cost − the need to also cause minimal environmental impact has been slow to form part of the promoter's Terms of Reference (TOR). However, towards the end of the twentieth century, environmental issues started to be represented in the TOR, and this led to the engagement of specialist advisers to investigate environmental impact, suggest alternative sites or options, or advise on mitigation − and here the ingenuity of engineers came into its own.

In the 1970s, as we have seen, Dame Sylvia Crowe advised on Rutland Water, the largest (in terms of surface area) manmade lake in England and Wales, constructed between 1971 and 1975 at Empingham to meet the expansion requirements of Peterborough, Corby, Northampton, Daventry and Wellingborough. Rutland Water, covering 1,260 hectares, was formed by a 40-metre-high earth embankment dam in the valley of the River Gwash and is filled by water pumped from the Welland and the Nene. It was promoted jointly by the Mid-Northamptonshire Water Board and the Welland and Nene River Authority since it incorporated river regulation as well as a water-supply source. Designed by Watson Hawksley together with Crowe, it was opposed by the Council for the Protection of Rural England, local authorities, the National Farmers Union and the Country Landowners Association principally on

landscape grounds and the potential loss of agricultural land. The site was selected in 1967 and received parliamentary approval in 1970.[18] A 'backstop' dam was built around Normanton Church, which was to stand incongruously in the reservoir – it is used today as a visitor centre.

The Kielder scheme in Northumberland, promoted at about the same time as Empingham, while at 1,000 hectares not covering the same surface area, is the largest reservoir in terms of capacity in England at 200,000,000 cubic metres. It was promoted at the end of the 1960s at a time of rapid economic and population growth, constructed in the 1970s, a decade of reduced growth, and finished at the start of the 1980s recession.[19] It was designed by Babtie, Shaw and Morton to meet the needs of British Steel's new steel-making complex at Redcar and new plants for the chemical industry. It was also vigorously opposed, and, being in an area of great natural beauty, planning conditions were imposed for its design and construction; it is used extensively for recreation. The backstop dam at Bakethin (similar in function to that at Rutland) was constructed as

Normanton Church preserved by a dam within Rutland Water.

part of this scheme for purely environmental reasons: it retains water and prevents exposure of mud when Kielder is drawn down.

Environmental awareness came too late at the Kariba Dam built in 1959 on the Zambezi on the borders of Zambia and Zimbabwe. The construction of the 128-metre-high arch dam formed a reservoir more than eight times the surface area of Lake Geneva. As the waters rose, the lives of the Batonka tribe — numbering some 40,000 — and the wildlife of the area were under threat. This triggered an early awareness of the potential environmental impacts of dams in the writer David Howarth: 'I had learned . . . about the effects of the environment on the building of the dam, but not so much about the effects of the dam on its environment.'[20]

The Batonka tribe were relocated to 800,000 hectares of land set aside for them as part of the scheme, which was achieved with some resignation on the part of the tribespeople. For the most part

Bakethin Dam – a backstop dam created within Kielder Water, Northumberland, in 1982 for environmental reasons.

they accepted the words of the Minister for Native Affairs (for Southern Rhodesia), Sir Patrick Fletcher, who came and sat in their villages and told them that the river was going to grow. (However, in Northern Rhodesia, eight tribesmen were shot in attempting to resist relocation.)

For the wildlife, no such explanation was forthcoming. What became known as 'Operation Noah' was mounted to save the animals of the forest and bush. The usefulness of this exercise has probably been exaggerated, but, regardless of its degree of success, Frank Clements pointed out that 'for every animal rescued by Operation Noah, at least two . . . have been shot by officials working to eradicate tsetse fly.'[21] It was estimated that 130,000 head of game were killed between 1953 and 1957. Animals were rescued by a small flotilla of boats, and the distance that they could swim unaided was discovered: waterbuck 3.2 kilometres, kudu antelope 1.6 kilometres, zebra 550 metres, baboon 365 metres. Ropes were

First Day Cover from Rhodesia and Nyasaland to commemorate the opening of Kariba Dam by Queen Elizabeth II in 1960. Today the reservoir marks the border between Zimbabwe and Zambia.

found to be causing injury to some of the larger animals as they were rescued, and the Society for the Prevention of Cruelty to Animals (SPCA) launched an appeal for old nylon stockings, which would not break the animals' skin. Within 24 hours a thousand pairs arrived; they continued to flood in from all over the world, with the overwhelmed SPCA now pleading for people to stop sending them (they were no longer needed but customs fees had to be paid for each pair!). In Northern Rhodesia, answering an appeal for an 'Animal Dunkirk' from the Central Africa Federation's *Sunday Mail*, an appeal was launched to 'the huntin' shootin' and fishin' set members of the Game Preservation and Hunting Association — the majority from Britain — to give up their holidays to save stranded animals'.[22] It will never be known how many animals died from starvation or drowned as Lake Kariba rose; 3,000, including birds, reptiles and small mammals, were rescued.

The most challenging scheme in terms of its environmental impact has been the High Aswan Dam in Egypt built in 1968. It was never going to be easy flooding the Nile Valley. The options taxed the brains of some of the most eminent engineers of the twentieth century. Fortunately, none of them took the view of Mohammed Ali in 1833 to build a dam at Cairo using the stones of the Pyramids!

Egypt occupies an area of a million square kilometres but only 39,000 are habitable: the 1,600-kilometre course of the Nile, which is only about 9 kilometres wide until it reaches Cairo and its delta. People have depended on it for food and drink for at least 6,000 years. It is fed by the White Nile (which flows into Lakes Victoria and Albert; they steady its flow to be consistent downstream to Egypt year round) and the Blue Nile from Ethiopia (which floods from June to August, bringing to Egypt its rich fertile silt). This is the annual miracle for the people of the valley whose task over the centuries has been to cause it to linger. The French introduced cotton to Egypt in the early nineteenth century, and Mohammed Ali, who had become viceroy to the Turkish Sultan in 1805, decided to grow it as a cash crop for export. This committed Egypt to perennial irrigation since cotton requires water in late spring and summer when the Nile is at its lowest.

Mohammed Ali built a barrage just to the south of Cairo to maintain a head of water to the delta in 1840, but it never worked properly until the British occupation of 1882, when Sir Colin Scott-Moncrieff repaired it. By 1890 it was capable of holding water to a depth of 4 metres. The British engineers were not satisfied with this and, as we have seen, proposed a new dam at Aswan, completed in 1902. It was so successful in boosting Egypt's prosperity that it was raised again in 1912. Demand for irrigation water from the increasing population continued to rise, and it was raised again in 1933 by 9 metres. (The Mohammed Ali barrage is now replaced in function by others on the Rosetta and Damietta branches of the river.)

However, Egypt was still dependent on the vagaries of the autumn rain, which could provide too much or too little. By 1962 the population was 25,000,000 and the Lower Nile Valley the most densely populated area in the world. From ancient times it had been able to support 7,000,000, but the virtues of civilization had caused it to be a victim of its own success. Improved medical services allowed more children to survive and diseases to be eradicated. As Tom Little put it, 'it was like saving a man from the gallows in order to starve him to death.' [23]

The British made Egypt one of the most fertile agricultural areas in the world, and by the time the first Aswan Dam was in operation the population stood at 12,000,000. But the prosperity couldn't last, and nothing the British did could keep pace with the rapidly rising population. At independence in 1936 the people were poorer than when the British had come. King Farouk fared even worse, and, despite

perennial irrigation, yields levelled off with decreased fertility and drainage. The national income was now being expended on fertilizer.

However, the country had no industrial base to support itself, largely due to lack of power, and the population in the low-lying areas of the delta were still subject to flooding. And so the concept of a High Dam at Aswan was born – this would store more water than would be needed in any one year, provide power and protect the populated areas from floods.

In 1901 William Willcocks had advocated the use of Lakes Victoria, Albert and Tana as storage and regulating reservoirs and the cutting of a canal through the southern swamps of Sudan, where half the flow of the White Nile was lost. When Gamal Abdel Nasser asked Britain to advise on maximizing the water available to Egypt, this was still the suggested option, and the Owen Falls Dam was built downstream of the exit of the river from Lake Victoria, making it the biggest reservoir in the world and a source of hydroelectric power for Uganda.

However, Nasser was a driven man and the High Dam became his pyramid. The question was how to fund it. Germany had agreed to pay Israel 3 billion marks as reparation for Jewish suffering in the

First Day Cover for the High Aswan Dam, 1960.

Second World War, and, in response to Arab protests that this strengthened their enemy, the Germans agreed to prepare the plans for the High Dam project. In order to build international confidence that it would be built, Nasser had white lines painted in the spring of 1955 on the banks of the Nile where the 'mountain of a dam' was to be built.

Subject to a favourable World Bank report on the economic benefits, Britain and America informed Egypt that they would offer loans for the first stage of the work. A consortium of Hochtief and Dortmund Union, Wimpey, BICC, British Electric and French firms was formed in September 1955. In February 1956 the World Bank offered £100,000,000, the US £55,000,000 and Britain £15,000,000 loans for the construction of the first stage. Nasser wanted a commitment for completion, but by this time relations had started to cool as a result of the 1955 Baghdad Pact, which he had seen as a diversion of arms to Iraq to defend Western interests against Russia rather than Egypt against Israel. Accordingly, he negotiated an arms deal with Czechoslovakia and, to make matters worse in Western eyes, recognized Communist China. Too late, in July 1956, he agreed to accept the loans only to find that the US and Britain had withdrawn their offers.

Nasser retaliated by nationalizing the Suez Canal Company to use the profits to fund the dam. The consortium was disbanded and the Suez Crisis ensued, with invasion of Egypt by the French and British. While the fiasco brought down the British Prime Minister Anthony Eden, it didn't do the High Dam much good, with Nasser's emissaries scouring the world for alternative funding while his white lines at Aswan began to fade. Japan, Italy and Germany showed interest, but inexorably the Egyptian economy was linked to Russia: in 1957 the Soviet bloc took 50 per cent of Egypt's foreign trade. In December 1958 a contract was signed for a Russian loan to begin construction on condition that Russian plant and equipment was used.

While the dam was to be built 320 kilometres to the north of the Egypt/Sudan border, the resulting reservoir was to flood 160 kilometres into Sudan – effectively the inhabited region of Sudanese Nubia with a population of 100,000. An agreement was reached by which Egypt paid the Sudan £E15,000,000 for resettlement of the Nubians and the net surplus water arising from the scheme was to be split 1:2 Egypt:Sudan.

On 9 January 1966, a further eight years and four million new Egyptians after he had decided to embark on the project, Nasser laid the foundation stone for the dam. So the die was cast for the people and their cultural heritage upstream. The 50,000 Nubians from Sudan were moved from Wadi Halfa to Atbura, albeit reluctantly. Egyptian Nubians numbering some 100,000, many of whom had moved each time the Aswan dams were developed, were to be moved to New Nubia at Kom Ombo 56 kilometres to the north of Aswan.

The Nile Valley in Egypt and Sudan is rich in temples, monuments, rock paintings, fortresses, ancient towns, churches and rock graves from ancient civilizations – as well as prehistory – all of which was now threatened by the inexorable rise of the waters of the High Dam lake. Archaeological investigations had proceeded with painstaking care since the plans had been initiated, but suddenly time was not on the side of research: 'The tide of history was being replaced by the flood of a reservoir.' Money had to be found, teams assembled and recording or rescue undertaken. It was possible to determine priorities with some accuracy since, as the lake started to rise in 1964, it would submerge monuments at increasingly higher levels until reaching its maximum height in 1970[24] – however, experts had to decide the order of salvation. For example, the temple of Kalabsha, 65 kilometres south of the dam, would be the first submerged. With the help of West Germany, it had been removed and recreated by 1963.

Contributions were forthcoming from all over the world. UNESCO launched a campaign to raise funds, but one offer from the Parker Pen Company to remove the temple of Dendur to Janesville, Wisconsin, was refused. The overall sum needed to protect or remove monuments was estimated in 1961 to be $87,000,000 of which $70,000,000 was needed for the rock temples at Abu Simbel, the charismatic jewel in the crown.

A rock-fill dam to be built around the temple to protect it from the lake was first proposed (at a cost of $82,000,000), but, apart from a continuous pumping cost, the aesthetics of the temple being below water level rather than set on their vantage point was not appealing. The second plan was to jack up the temples in two blocks from the riverside 70 metres to the top of the hill – at a cost of $63,000,000 – on 250 hydraulic jacks a millimetre at a time. This caused disquiet among some members of the UN who considered that the education of children (another UNESCO remit) was preferable to saving monuments. William MacQuity, a film producer, in collaboration with the engineers Ove Arup, proposed that the temples be preserved under water. They would be surrounded by a membrane into which lifts, restaurants and viewing areas would be installed with the water being purified to remain clear. Although this scheme would have only cost £2,000,000 to build, it was summarily rejected on the grounds that turning archaeology into a goldfish bowl was not worthy of consideration. Another scheme was to 'float' the temples to the top of the hill on floating foundations and then move them to a prepared site and remake the landscape around them. At a cost of £35,000,000 it was rejected because the cost was thought to be greatly underestimated.

The appeal failed to raise the funds in time so an Egyptian plan

to cut up the monuments and move them to the top of the hill at a cost of $32,000,000 was proposed and a contract signed in November 1963. Funds for the exercise were provided by 45 countries (with Britain's parsimonious £200,000 exceeded by contributions by a number of countries such as India, Holland, Italy and Spain – was Britain still smarting at Suez?). The Egyptian plan was executed with the temples cut into slabs, each block numbered, waterproofed, lifted by 30-ton cranes and reassembled.

Whereas vast resources and efforts to protect culture from the results of a dam can be made, Venice presents the opportunity to protect culture by *means* of a dam.

Venice has always relied on the sea for its independence. However, the balance between the sea's role as a protector of the city and its potential as a threat is precarious: 'Now that protection *by* water is no longer required, protection *from* water has become a key factor in the city's survival.[25] Building subsidence and rising sea levels now mean that the city is flooded with increasing frequency.

Venice currently experiences flooding on 200 days each year

The temple of Abu Simbel in its latest resting place on the banks of Lake Nasser.

compared with only seven at the beginning of the twentieth century; in 1966 a flood left 5000 people homeless. Since then, an endless round of debate and argument finally resulted in approval of the 'Moses' (Modal Sperimentale Elettromeccanico) scheme in 2003. The plans propose 79 hinged flood barriers on the seabed

Abu Simbel being moved in 1964.

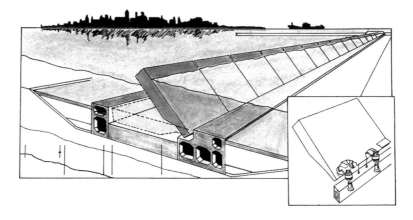

which will be raised when high tides threaten the city. Buoyancy tanks inside the gates will normally be filled with water, but, when a high tide is expected, compressed air will be pumped into the gates causing them to rise. Each gate will be up to 30 metres high and, once raised, will form a barrier against the incoming tide. Four barrier systems will be built by 2011 to protect the lagoon and the historic city with its unique network of canals. While opposed by a proportion of navigation interests and ecologists, the Governor of Veneto said in 2005 that Venice could suffer the fate of New Orleans if the project did not go ahead. A hundred and fifty years ago, John Ruskin highlighted the threat to Venice by 'modernizers'. With those lessons learned, the city at last has the promise of being protected from the elements and the vagaries of climate change for a few more hundred years.

After the Second World War and the realization of the benefits of the TVA in America, a sea change began to occur in the environmental approach to the development of dam schemes. In Britain, the North Wales Hydroelectricity Act 1952 required landscape architects to be involved in project design, and the tide turned in 1960 when

The Moses Gates designed to protect Venice from the tides and rising sea levels.

Frederick Gibberd addressed the Institution of Water Engineers in London. He assisted with the Kielder Reservoir in Northumberland, opened in 1981. At the time of his paper he had been involved with the design of the Derwent Reservoir in Durham and the Tryweryn in North Wales. He maintained – to an audience of engineers – that a reservoir scheme should be built to a 'standard of comeliness and decency, and that we should not get it without a landscape architect as a member of the team'.[26]

The involvement of architects as such in reservoir creation – Gibberd said that 'nature herself will be the landscape consultant for the shape of the lake' – was not new, as had been apparent at the Hoover Dam in the 1930s. But involvement on a regular basis was still the exception rather than the rule. One exception was the employment of Barbara Frears (née Wallhouse) as an architect on the Staunton Harold Reservoir for the River Dove Water Board in Leicester in 1956. At the inauguration of the scheme in 1960, even the contractor remarked that, rather than the customary 'Waterworks Baronial' architecture, he was pleased that a thing of real beauty had been created.

From the 1960s onwards the design teams for dams grew – first

Sketches of the proposed Valve Tower for Staunton Harold reservoir, Leicestershire.

Completed Valve Tower, Staunton Harold, c. 1965.

with landscape architects and then, as environmental assessment legislation required more specialist involvement, with ecologists, fisheries experts and archaeologists, as well as town and country planners. A similar series of dynasties developed among these specialists as had occurred in the engineering profession in the nineteenth century. Dame Sylvia Crowe was the landscape advisor for Bough Beech reservoir in 1965, Bewl Water in 1975, Ardingly in 1977 and Rutland Water, completed in 1975. The first scheme for Broad Oak in Kent was promoted with the landscape advice of Colvin and Moggridge in 1976; the second scheme had the advice of Nicholas Pearson Associates in 1990. The landscape planner Nicholas Pearson was involved in the design of the award-winning Megget Scheme as well as proposed reservoir developments in London, Kent and Devon. Creation of water-supply reservoirs in Hampshire with Rofe, Kennard and Lapworth resulted in environmental awards, and they were eventually designated as SSSIs, a Special Protection Area

Megget Reservoir embankment dam, Scotland, selected by the viewing public for BBC Design of the Year Award, 1987.

under the EU Wild Birds Directive and a Ramsar site. For all these schemes an ever-wider range of specialists was retained, including terrestrial and aquatic ecologists and archaeologists.

The environmental effects of dams were considered by Mansergh in his design parameters for the Elan Valley dams in the 1890s: he paid particular attention to the need to maintain river flows *downstream* of them. It was noted that the Nile delta's accretion was reversed with the construction of the first delta barrage in 1868. Despite these early lessons, at the end of the twentieth century we still had not fully taken these lessons on board. The Three Gorges Dam illustrates this point.

China has been thought by some to exhibit contradictions;[27] the approach to development is a typical case. There are currently plans for a new 'sustainable' city to be built on Chongming Island in the mouth of the Yangtze downstream from Shanghai. The island has grown from the sediments brought down by melt-water from the Himalayas which has deposited the silt at the Yangtze's mouth: today its wetlands are home to and a breeding ground for thousands of wild cranes, swans and wildfowl.

Meanwhile the Chinese government recognizes that the country is on the edge of an environmental abyss: economic growth has been achieved at a price. Taking 250,000,000 rural peasants out of poverty has resulted in environmental degradation not seen since the Industrial Revolution in the West; a new coal-fired power station is built every 10 days. China is now predicted to be the largest emitter of greenhouse gases in the world. According to Deputy Environment Minister Pan Yue, the economic miracle cannot continue because the environment can no longer keep pace: 'five of the ten most polluted cities in the world are in China; half of the water in our seven major rivers is useless . . . ' The 11th Five-year Plan unveiled by Premier Wen Jiabao in 2006 decreed that growth must now be sustainable – with reductions in pollutants emitted and in total energy and water use. As a consequence, new development is required to have the same ecological footprint as a traditional Chinese village.

The eco-city of Dongtan ('eastern sandbank' in Mandarin) on Chongming Island is intended as a demonstration project of such developments with targets of zero-emission transport and to be run entirely on renewable energy. This is all very laudable, and as an exemplar it is fulfilling its purpose – Arups, the designers of Dongtan, have been commissioned to plan three more eco-demonstrator cities. However, what the Himalayas provide, the Three Gorges Dam can take away. An island that was created naturally from the silt-laden waters of the Yangtze may not be sustainable if that very silt is trapped behind a dam 1000 kilometres upstream. Coupled with the potential for ground level to no longer be replenished is the small matter of rising sea levels – already Dongtan is going to need flood walls 8 metres high to protect its 3-metre above sea level ground level from the waves. (We may wonder what height they will need to be in the event of a Hurricane Katrina hitting the Shanghai coast.) The problems don't end there: fisheries in the East China Sea are threatened due to the reduction in nutrients brought by the Yangtze, and wetlands in the estuary which are havens for wildfowl and waders are in danger of disappearing as the sediment reduces.[28] It is also feared that the harbour of Chongqing, for which the dam is designed to facilitate navigation, will silt up as a result of its construction.[29]

To address these issues, the engineers believe that they have learned from experience elsewhere: other rivers, notably the Yellow, carry a much larger silt load which has caused problems when the rivers have been dammed. Half the annual silt in the Yangtze is carried in the months between July and September, and it is planned to discharge the silt at this time through the 23 bottom outlet gates in the Three Gorges Dam. The silt flow will be concentrated in the middle of the river channel, which will help to discharge the silt through the sluices.[30] Only time will tell if this plan will be successful.

While the Three Gorges Project has been one of the most controversial schemes in the world, the promoters maintain that it is aimed at improving the ecology and environment along the Yangtze. The Yangtze *has* caused serious loss of life and property, and the project can be promoted on grounds of flood defence alone, given that these disasters have constrained sustainable economic development, but the issue is compounded by the fact that, with the rapid increase in population in the valley, this in turn has intensified pressure on the environment and natural resources. Forests have been cut down, increasingly sloping land has been cultivated – which has led to water and soil erosion.[31] Studies have been carried out for many years, and it is recognized by the promoters that there will be more sedimentation upstream, fisheries will change (including in the East China Sea), water quality will reduce, and historic sites will be inundated; the aquatic ecology will undoubtedly change in both the reservoir and the river itself. However, the flood control will protect bank-side ecology and improve flows and quality downstream. The TGP Corporation still contends that the main environmental benefit from the project is that the generation of hydropower will reduce the emissions that would otherwise result from coal-fired plants (or the waste from nuclear power stations).

Over recent years, design engineers and their teams have become adept at overcoming many of the problems that have beset schemes in the past. Spillways have been designed to retain or flush out sediment. Fish passes – such as fish ladders or fish locks – allow

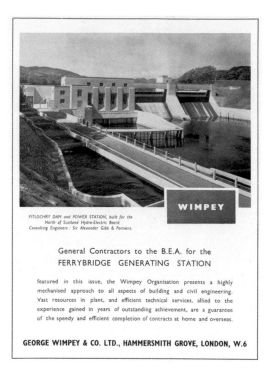
adult fish to swim upstream to spawn and back downstream with their young; it is essential to design the pass appropriate to the target species. Chip Ward has said 'if dams are icons of progress, salmon have become sacramental totems of wild rivers.'[32] At the Haweswater Dam fish passes were added in the 1960s with extra water being allowed out of the reservoir during the winter to assist the salmon on their journey. Health-impact assessments are advised by the World Health Organization and WCD to assess the viability of a project prior to construction. Properly undertaken, this can ensure that there is no repetition of the vector-borne diseases associated with tropical schemes in the past.

So, at the end of the twentieth century considerable attention was being paid to the environmental design – and operation – of dams. Not only was there guidance from practitioners and the

A Wimpey advert showing the fish pass at Pitlochry hydroelectric scheme, Scotland.

values and priorities of the WCD, but there was legislative pressure and, perhaps most important of all, insistence from funders and promoters on environmental enhancement through design. Dam engineers responded to this pressure. The Code of Ethics of ICOLD acknowledges that existing dams were designed at a time when less knowledge was available about the environmental impacts of dams: there is now room for improvement. The Code specifically requires commitments to operating life, social impacts, environment and safety.[33] Recognizing that dams 'have both positive and negative impacts on the environment', ICOLD professionals commit to ensuring that the positive outweigh the negative impacts and to assess the extent of the environmental impact. As we have seen, the challenge facing them should not be underestimated.

Two girls have a final look at their home town, shortly to be submerged by the Three Gorges Dam project, 2003.

Assorted dams on foreign bank-notes.

Postscript

This has been a story about dams. It has meandered like an untamed river through tales of the men and women who designed, promoted, opposed and built some of the most fantastic structures on earth.

The results have not always been as intended – indeed the wheel has now turned full circle, and dams are being dismantled as more efficient means of providing the services they offered are discovered and implemented. And they have to be dismantled because, as we have seen, they rarely fail of their own accord.

It has been demonstrated that dams are in fact entirely natural phenomena. Perhaps drawing on examples from nature, early peoples built dams to store water to drink, for irrigation against dry seasons or years, and to manage the risks of flooding and drought. The young John Muir built dams on his farm stream. Winston Churchill may not have been entirely ahead of his time when he wished 'the Nile to perish before it reached the sea', but he did see it as 'flowing through smiling countries', bringing life and sustenance along its way. With the world's current population, dams are here to stay, and have a rightful and important part to play in our sustainable infrastructure. They provide us with drinking water, protect us from floods, irrigate our fields and, perhaps most crucially, produce clean, renewable energy at a time when fossil fuels are diminishing and nuclear energy produces waste that cannot be disposed of. Dams will also be able to address the need for more water for agriculture that climate change will bring. However, they bring problems with them when they are built in the wrong place, for the wrong reasons and without proper consideration of operation and design.

In retrospect they have been made possible by technological advances as well as administrative co-ordination and direction. Different societies have reacted in different ways with, for example, the British and the French going in opposite directions (but being more adventurous in their colonies) and the Americans providing big dams to control big rivers. Fred Pearce, while admitting to a sneaking love of large dams, maintained that they have 'proved [to be] an exceptionally effective technology for turning the unruly flow of rivers into private or state property'.[1]

The 'big dam' vision was based on the premise of conquest: the bigger the river, the bigger the challenge to be met. It was epitomized by the Hoover Dam, which marked a turning point: the coming of the era of the mega-dam and mega-project involving schemes for whole river basins or basin transfer. The number of dams being built peaked in the 1960s, but, while fewer dams have been constructed since then, they are now much larger and create vast reservoirs. From being the largest dam in the world in the 1930s, the Hoover Dam now does not rank in the top 30. In terms of electricity generated it isn't in the top 100. These mega-structures have sustained life and increasing populations, but, with a growing awareness of the need for longer-term management of our natural resources, questions have been raised. Are dams a false dawn for civilization? Are we raising our expectations regarding the population the earth can sustain?

The WCD took evidence from all sides, (almost) reached a consensus on the way forward and developed a set of principles. Since the publication of their report in 2000, it has been encouraging that some countries, notably China, have re-evaluated schemes in terms of environmental and social impact. Most existing dams worldwide were designed between 1950 and 1970, when there was little concern for the environment; with a heightened awareness by all parties, impacts can be addressed. There remain those that obstinately pursue an economic dream, refusing to learn the lessons of history. Many problems are caused by the intransigence of the few refusing to acknowledge that those affected have rights and should be treated fairly.

But with fossil fuels inevitably diminishing, the scope for greater delivery of (renewable) hydroelectricity has to be recognized. Currently it contributes only 5 per cent of the world's electricity generation; it can be argued that the world is less polluted than in the heyday of dam construction in the 1960s, but global warming has taken the place of pollution as the environment's nemesis. Hydroelectricity, provided it is developed on sustainable principles, may be the earth's saviour. At present, only 1 per cent of Africa's hydropower potential is used.[2] Belatedly, the World Bank adopted a policy of environmental assessment of proposed dam and reservoir projects. Smaller-scale schemes have gained currency in some areas; the American Corps of Engineers have had to present non-structural alternatives to proposed water projects since 1986. Economies of scale and operation, security and multi-functionalism probably indicate that there will continue to be a place for properly administered large-scale schemes, however – even replacing decommissioned smaller dams.

A policy of dam development based on the criteria heralded by Mansergh and Rawlinson over a century ago and teams incorporating social and environmental scientists may well lead to the truly sustainable dam. Just as dam engineers had a low profile so it has been with dams – until they appear in our backyard. Hopefully the stories recounted in this book will assure planners, engineers and environmentalists alike that, 'Frankly, we *do* give a Dam.'

Glossary

Aqueduct An artificial channel to carry water.

Aquifer Underground water-bearing geological stratum that can be used as a source of water if tapped by a well or borehole.

Barrage The French term for a dam or weir but commonly used in English for a large diversion dam, especially on rivers in Egypt and India or in estuaries.

Borrow Pit Excavation for material to construct an earth dam. Often sited within area of resulting reservoir.

Bund Term for embankment or dyke commonly used in the Far East and India.

Bypass This takes a number of forms, such as fish-passes or ladders to permit the passage of migratory fish, or locks and canals for shipping on navigable waterways.

Cataract Shallows in a river where rapids with rocky outcrops are found.

Contour-canal A navigable waterway built along one level and therefore requiring no locks.

Core wall The central, watertight wall of an earth or rock dam. Originally puddle clay was the material of construction; now concrete is often used.

Cut-off trench A deep excavation under the full length of a dam filled with an impervious material – puddle clay or concrete – designed to prevent or inhibit seepage under the structure.

Dams

  Arch dam Usually made of concrete in the form of a horizontal arch that transfers the stresses or loads to the valley sides into which they are keyed. These are suited to steep-sided valleys where maximum strength is provided with minimum volume. Arch dams are thin structures and require less material than any other type to build.

  Buttress dam One in which a series of cantilevers, slabs, arches or domes forms the water face and is supported on its air face by a line of triangular walls called buttresses. They combine economy of concrete with stability. Each section with its buttress acts as a gravity dam.

  Coffer dam A temporary dam built to exclude water from a construction site.

  Diversion dam A dam built across a river to divert water into a canal or aqueduct. It raises the level of a river but does not provide any storage volume.

  Double curvature or cupola dam In wider valleys with gently sloping sides, the stresses near the centre of the arch may become excessive and, to withstand this, the wall is designed with a vertical as well as a horizontal curvature.

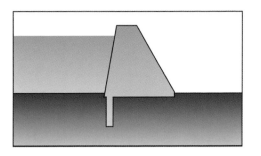

Gravity dam.

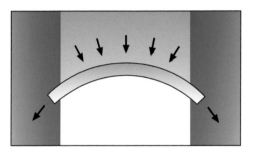

Arch dam.

Cupola dam.

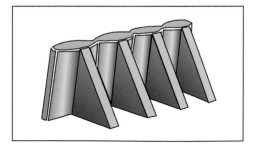

Buttress Dam.

Earth dam A massive earthen bank with sloping faces and made watertight, or nearly so, with a core wall and, usually, an impervious water-face membrane.

Embankment dams Frequently earth or rockfill embankments of low permeability having a flexible impermeable core, usually of clay, to resist seepage. Rockfill dams may have an impervious water face membrane. Usually selected for sites with wide valleys and can be built on rock or softer soils.

Gravity dam Uses masonry or concrete that resists the applied water load by means of its weight.

Dyke A word widely used in northern Europe for two different things. It can mean 'a ditch or channel used for drainage' *or* 'a wall or bank used for flood protection'.

Environmental Impact Assessment A system of assessing the environmental impacts of development. Initiated in the US from the 1960s and formalized as a European Union Directive in 1985.

Glacial trough A valley, sometimes very large, cut by the movement of a glacier.

Leat A channel taken from a river to direct the flow to a water-wheel or turbine.

Levee An embankment alongside a river which prevents flooding.

Moraines Rock material that is carried, or has been carried and then deposited, by a glacier.

Penstock A channel taking water from a reservoir to a water-wheel or, in modern times, a turbine.

Piping This occurs when the force exerted on the soil in or under an earth dam by water seeping through it is greater than the soil's capacity to resist being washed away.

Polder Land reclaimed from the sea, a marsh or an inland sea.

Pore-water pressure The pressure developed in the pores of a material due to the presence of seeping water.

Puddled clay Unworked clay is not watertight; if it is mixed with the right amount of sand, wetted and kneaded or tamped, it is called 'puddle clay' and will serve as an excellent watertight lining so long as it is kept wet.

Qanat An underground channel that intercepts an aquifer like a horizontal well.

Riparian Of, or related to, a river. Riparian ownership refers to rights as a result of owning land next to a river.

Spillway This permits the controlled escape of excess water in times of flood, particularly for embankment dams, which can be scoured or breached by uncontrolled water pouring over the top. Spillways can provide (1) release over the top of the dam; (2) overflow via a side channel to the dam; (3) overflow via a bell-mouth within the reservoir to the air face of the dam.

Summit-level canal A canal that crosses high ground. Such waterways are fitted with pound-locks and a summit-level water supply usually provided from a reservoir.

Tank Any water-storing structure, on or below ground level, and ranging in size from the very small to the huge tanks of Sri Lanka and India, many kilometres in circumference.

Uplift Water percolating underneath a structure exerts upward pressure, potentially raising that structure.

Weir A river dam used to raise the level so as to divert water into a canal, penstock or leat.

Valve tower Set within the reservoir or integrated into the dam, they are designed to draw off water for supply purposes as near to the surface as possible thus decanting the purer water, and so they have a range of inlets at different levels.

References

Introduction

1 James Mansergh, writing in an illustrated booklet presented to the owners of land submerged by his Elan Valley Reservoir scheme (R. Eustace Tickell, *The Vale of Nantgwillt: A Submerged Valley* [London, 1894]), p. 15.
2 John Muir, *The Yosemite* (New York, 1912 [2003]), p. 259.
3 Large dams are defined by the International Commission on Large Dams (ICOLD) as being more than 15 metres high from the foundation to the crest.
4 Endorsement of Hoover Dam project by Senate Committee, 1928.
5 David Constantine, *Under the Dam* (Manchester, 2005).
6 Arundhati Roy, *The Cost of Living* (Toronto, 1999), p. 8.
7 World Commission on Dams (WCD), *Dams and Development: A New Framework for Decision-Making* (London, 2000).
8 V. I. Lenin, *On the Development of Heavy Industry and Electrification* (Moscow, 1972).
9 Winston S. Churchill, *The River War* (London, 1899), in Herbert Addison, *Sun and Shadow at Asusan* (London, 1959), p. 45.
10 Patrick McCully, *Silenced Rivers* (1996; London, 2001), p. 72.

1 Dam as Symbol and Function

1 F. L. Jones, *The Letters of Percy Bysshe Shelley* (Oxford, 1964), p. 283. Shelley himself would not necessarily have been averse to the dams since in 1812 he had lent his support to a scheme to dam the estuary at Tremadoc in North Wales.
2 E. L. Mansergh and W. L. Mansergh, *The Works for the Supply of Water to the City of Birmingham from Mid Wales, Proceedings of the ICE [Institution of Civil Engineers]*, 190 (1912), pp. 23–5.
3 'Birmingham Water Bill', *Birmingham Daily Post*, 7 March 1892.
4 'The Vyrnwy Lake of the Liverpool Waterworks', *Illustrated London News*, 23 February 1889.
5 Emlyn Williams, *The Last Days of Dolwyn* (London Film Studios, 1949).
6 Bijan Farhangi, *Contemporary Dam Construction in Iran* (Teheran, 1998), p. 21.
7 George Nathaniel Curzon (Lord Curzon of Kedleston), *Persia and the Persian Problem* (London, 1892).

8 Karl Wittfogel, *Oriental Despotism* (New Haven, CT, 1957), cited in Fred Pearce, *The Dammed* (London, 1992), p. 13.

9 Donald Worster, *Hoover Dam: A Study in Domination* (New York, 1972), cited in Donald C. Jackson, *Dams: Studies in the History of Civil Engineering* (Aldershot, 1997), p. 343.

10 Peter Speed, *Dorset: A County History* (Newbury, 1994), p. 138.

11 Binnie & Partners, *Mangla* (London, 1971), p. 12.

12 Dai Qing, *The River Dragon Has Come!* (New York, 1998), foreword, p. xx.

13 Fred Pearce, *The Dammed* (London, 1992), p. 117.

14 Calvin Coolidge, 'Address to the American Society of Newspaper Editors', 25 January 1925.

15 Pearce, *The Dammed* (London, 1992), p. 68.

16 Norman Smith, *A History of Dams* (London, 1971), p. 207.

17 *Ibid*, p. 221.

18 Samuel Smiles, *Lives of the Engineers* (London, 1862), p. 238.

19 Thomas Telford to James Jardine, 7 April 1821, ICE Archives.

20 Nicholas Schnitter, *A History of Dams: The Useful Pyramids* (Rotterdam, 1994), p. 151.

21 L.A.B. Wade, 'Concrete and Masonry Dam Construction in New South Wales', *Proc. ICE,* CLXXVIII (1909), pp. 1−110.

22 Smith, *A History of Dams*, p. 184.

23 'The New Croton Dam: New York City's Water Supply', *Scientific American* (20 January 1900).

24 Smith, *A History of Dams*, p. 216.

25 *Ibid*, p. 217.

26 Eva Jakobsson, *The Industrialization of Rivers* (Göteburg, 1996), p. 288.

27 Smith, *A History of Dams*, p. 234.

28 Itaipu Binacional, *Itaipu Hydroelectric Project* (Rio de Janeiro, 1981).

29 G. T. Pope, 'The Seven Wonders of the Modern World', *Popular Mechanics*, vol. 172 (December 1995), pp. 48–56.

30 Thames Barrage Association, *Dam the Thames: A Plan for a Tideless River in London* (1935).

31 'Three Gorges: The Biggest Dam in the World', Discovery Channel, 1998.

32 WWF, *To Dam or Not to Dam?* (Godalming, 2005) (the WWF's review of dams five years on from the World Commission on Dams), p. 12.

33 Julian Huxley, *TVA: Adventure in Planning* (Cheam, 1943). Writing in wartime Britain, Huxley was enthusiastic about the prospects of post-war planning in Europe reflecting the approach of the TVA as part of Roosevelt's New Deal, p. 53.

34 *Ibid*, p. 135.

35 David E. Lilienthal, *TVA Tennessee Valley Authority: Democracy on the March* (Middlesex, 1944), p.11. A director of the TVA from its inception in 1933, Lilienthal focused on the programme's social and economic benefits.

36 Huxley, *TVA*, p. 75.

37 Alan Ervine, Professor of Engineering, Glasgow University. Personal communication with the author.

2 Dam Designers and Builders

1 Samuel Smiles, *Lives of the Engineers*, 5 vols (London, 1862).
2 Angus Buchanan, *The Engineers – A History of the Engineering Profession in Britain 1750–1914* (London, 1989).
3 L.T.C. Rolt, *Victorian Engineering* (1970; Middlesex, 1988).
4 John Taverner, 'Certaine Experiments concerning Fish and Fruite: Practised by John Taverner Gentleman, and by him published for the benefit of others' (1600: Manchester, 1928).
5 Alan Skempton, ed., *John Smeaton FRS* (London, 1981), p. 75.
6 Buchanan, *The Engineers*, p. 51.
7 Nicholas Schnitter, *A History of Dams: The Useful Pyramids* (Rotterdam, 1994), p. 158.
8 Geoffrey Binnie, *Early Victorian Water Engineers* (London, 1981), p. 15.
9 Pedro Bernardo Villareal de Berriz, *Maquinas Hydraulicas de Malinas y herrerias* (Vizcaya, 1736: 1973)
10 Hugh Sutherland, 'Rankine: His Life and Times', Lecture delivered to the British Geotechnical Society at the University of Glasgow in December 1972 to mark the centenary of Rankine's death. (London, 1973), p. 11.
11 *Ibid.*, p. 17.
12 A. T. Mackenzie, *History of the Periyar Project* (Madras, 1899). Mackenzie was Executive Engineer of the Madras Public Works Department, p. 34.
13 A. Mohanakrishan, *History of the Periyar Dam* (New Delhi, 1997), p. 19.
14 *Ibid.*, p. 21.
15 Mackenzie, *History of the Periyar Project*, p. 116.
16 *Ibid.*, p. 123.
17 *Ibid.*, p. 124.
18 Robert Rawlinson, *Birmingham Water Supply: Report on the Public and Domestic Supply of Water to Birmingham to the Birmingham Corporation* (1871).
19 *Ibid.*
20 James Mansergh, Proof of Evidence in Support of the Water Bill, Birmingham Corporation, 1892.
21 Rita Morton, *The Building of the Elan Valley Dams* (Walsall, 1996), p. 66. Morton was a Schools and Visitors Liaison Officer for Severn Trent Water Authority in Birmingham and saved old records on privatization of Britain's water industry in 1989.
22 E. A. Lees, *A Description of the Works* (Birmingham, 1908), p. 6.
23 F. L. Jones, ed., *The Letters of Percy Bysshe Shelley*, vols I and II (Oxford 1964), p. 118.
24 *Ibid.*, pp. 119–20.
25 R. Eustace Tickell, *The Vale of Nantgwilt: A Submerged Valley* (London, 1894), p. 7.
26 *Ibid.*, p. 8.
27 *Ibid.*, pp. 11–15.
28 Thomas Barclay, *The Future Water Supply of Birmingham* (Birmingham, 1891), p. 114.
29 E. L. Mansergh and W. L. Mansergh, 'The Works for the Supply of Water to the City of Birmingham from Mid-Wales', *Proc. ICE*, CLXL (1912).
30 *Ibid.*
31 *Ibid.*
32 Morton, *The Building*, p. 7.
33 Dick Sullivan, *Navvyman* (Eye, 1983), p. 22.

34 *Ibid.*, p. 48. Sullivan's father was a navvy and his mother was born at the village hospital at Elan Valley in 1900.

35 H. D. Morgan, P. A. Scott, R.J.C. Walton, R. H. Falkiner, 'The Claerwen Dam', *Proc. ICE*, vol. 2.

36 Norman Smith, *The Centenary of the Aswan Dam 1902–2002* (London, 2002) (booklet to accompany an exhibition at the ICE in London to mark the inauguration of the dam on 10 December 1902), p. 1.

37 *Ibid.*, p. 8.

38 Fred Pearce, *The Dammed: Rivers, Dams and the Coming World Water Crisis* (London, 1992), p. 80.

39 Smith, *The Centenary*, p. 12.

40 Churchill, *The River War*, p. 43.

41 Smith, *The Centenary*, p. 47.

42 *Ibid.*, p. 51.

43 Pearce, *The Dammed*, p. 245.

44 David Billington, *The Tower and the Bridge: The New Art of Structural Engineering* (New York, 1983).

45 Donald C. Jackson, *Building the Ultimate Dam: John S. Eastwood and the Control of Water in the West* (Lawrence, KS, 1995), p. 123.

46 *Ibid.*, pp. 107.

47 *Ibid.*, p. 123.

48 *Ibid.*, p. 122.

49 *Ibid.*, p. 212.

50 *Ibid.*, p. 215.

51 *Ibid.*, p. 238.

52 W. H. Carson, *The Dam Builders: The Story of the Men Who Built Silent Valley Reservoir* (Newcastle, County Down, 1981), p. 75.

53 Bruce Murkoff, *Waterborne* (New York, 2004) (a novel based on the experiences of the builders of the Hoover Dam).

54 H. M. Newell, *The Dam* (London, 1956), p. 20 (a novel based on the experiences of the builders of the Grand Coulee Dam).

55 Woody Guthrie, *Roll on Columbia* (Bethleham, PA, 1991).

56 James Miller, *The Dam Builders: Power from the Glens* (Edinburgh, 2002), p. 20.

57 Emma Wood, *The Hydro Boys: Pioneers of Renewable Energy* (Edinburgh, 2002), p. 2.

58 Christine McCulloch, 'Political Ecology of Dams in Teesdale', in *Long Term Benefits and Performance of Dams* (London, 2004), pp. 49–66.

59 Marc Reisner, *Cadillac Desert: The American West and Its Disappearing Water* (London, 1990), p. 231.

60 Chip Ward, *Hope's Horizon: Three Visions for Healing this American Land* (Washington, DC, 2004), p. 126.

61 Reisner, *Cadillac Desert*, p. 263.

62 Schnitter, *A History of Dams*, p. 167.

3 Dam Beauty and Dam Proud

1 David Bindman, *Hogarth* (London, 1981).

2 William Hogarth, 'The Analysis of Beauty' (1753), in E. Malins, *English*

Landscaping and Literature 1660–1840 (London, 1966), p. 86.

3 Kenneth Woodbridge, *The Stourhead Landscape* (London, 1982), p. 53. Woodbridge quotes Dr Richard Pococke as saying in July 1754 that 'two pieces of water...are to be made into one . . . for which a head [dam] is making.'

4 Robert Farquhar, Bart., *Objections to the Thirlmere Scheme* (Ambleside, 1879).

5 Margaret Bourke-White, *Portrait of Myself* (London, 1964), p. 40.

6 Guy Cooper *et al.*, *English Water Gardens*, foreword Geoffrey Jellicoe (London, 1987), p. 7.

7 F. W. Robins, *The Story of Water Supply* (Oxford, 1946), p. 85.

8 R.C.S. Walters, *The Nation's Water Supply* (London, 1936), p. 192.

9 Delwyn G. Davies, *The Haweswater Dam* (Liverpool, 1940).

10 Tom Turner, *Landscape Planning* (London, 1987), p. 11.

11 *Ibid.*, p. 27.

12 T. Williams, *A History of Technology*, Vol. VII: *The 20th Century 1900–1950* (Part II) (Oxford, 1978). F. E. Bruce, Part 1 Water Supply, p. 1368.

13 Donald C. Jackson, *Great American Bridges and Dams* (New York, 1988), p. 243.

14 Charles Fowler, *Ideals of Engineering Architecture* (Chicago, 1929), p. 243.

15 *Ibid.*, p. 251.

16 W. O. Skeat, ed., *Manual of British Water Engineering Practice* (originally published 1950 as A. T. Hobbs, ed., *Manual of British Water Supply Practice*), third edn (Cambridge, 1961).

17 Oscar Faber, *The Aesthetic Aspect of Civil Engineering Design* (London, 1945), p. 11.

18 Charles Holden, *The Aesthetic Aspect of Civil Engineering Design* (London, 1945), p. 27.

19 *Ibid.*, p. 31.

20 Patrick Abercrombie, *The Aesthetic Aspect of Civil Engineering Design* (London, 1945), p. 73.

21 Skeat, *Manual*, p. 38.

22 Frederick Gibberd, 'The Landscape of Reservoirs', *Journal of the Institution of Water Engineers*, vol. 15 (1961), pp. 83–115.

23 A. C. Twort, D. D. Ratnayaka and M. J. Brandt, *Water Supply*, fifth edn (Oxford, 2000; reprinted 2002), p. 172.

24 Turner, *Landscape Planning*, p. 47.

25 Geoffrey A. Jellicoe, 'Water', in A. E. Weddle, ed., *Techniques of Landscape Architecture* (London, 1967), pp. 127–42.

26 D. G. Thornley, 'Water', in A. E. Weddle, ed., *Landscape Techniques* (London, 1979), pp. 119–40.

27 Thornley, in Weddle, *Landscape Techniques*, p. 134.

28 Michael Kennard and R. Reader, 'Cow Green Dam and Reservoir: J. Knill in Discussion', *Proc. ICE*, Part 1, vol. 60 (1976), pp. 461–74.

29 D. Coats and N. Ruffle, 'The Kielder Water Scheme' *Proc. ICE*, LXXII (1982); discussion LXXIV (1983), pp. 127–48.

30 ICOLD, *Dams in the UK* (London, 1983), p. 112.

31 Derek Lovejoy, ed., *Land Use and Landscape Planning* (Aylesbury, 1973), p. 203.

32 Turner, *Landscape Planning*, p. 48.

33 ICOLD, *Dams in the UK*, p. 160.

34 Brenda Colvin, *Land and Landscape* (1947; London, 1970), p. 341.

35 *Ibid.*, p. 343.

36 Sylvia Crowe, *Tomorrow's Landscape* (London, 1956), p. 38.

37 *Ibid.*, p. 158.

38 *Ibid.*, p. 60.

39 Tom Turner, *Landscape Planning and Environmental Impact Design* second edn (London, 1998), p. 397.

40 Twort *et al.*, *Water Supply*, p. 177.

41 Ed Gosschalk, *Reservoir Engineering: Guidelines for Practice* (London, 2002), p. 224.

42 *Ibid.*, p. 233.

43 D. Saslavsky, *Dnieprostroi: The Biggest Dam in the World* (Moscow, 1932), p. 10.

44 *Ibid.*, p. 33.

45 Isaac Deutscher, *The Prophet Unarmed: Trotsky: 1921–1929* (Oxford. 1959).

46 Saslavsky, *Dnieprostroi*, pp. 54–9.

47 Anna Louise Strong, *Wild River* (Boston, 1943), p. 4. Strong was born in Nebraska and went to the Soviet Union in 1921 as a member of a relief mission. She started the *Moscow Daily News* in 1930. In *Wild River* she tells the story of the building and destruction of the Dneiper Dam.

48 Alexander Danilevsky, 'Dams in the Soviet Union', in *Dams in Europe & USSR* (Paris, 1990), p. 105.

49 Alan Sillitoe, *Road to Volgograd* (London, 1964), p. 124.

50 V. M. Serebryanskii, 'The Architecture of Dams', in *Power Technology & Engineering*, IX/10 (October 1975).

51 Julian Huxley, *TVA: Adventure in Planning* (Cheam, 1943), p. 76.

52 Patrick McCully, *Silenced Rivers* (1996; London, 2001), p. 2.

53 Pandit Nehru, *Social Aspects of Small and Big Projects: Science and Society* (New Delhi, 1988).

54 'Prime Ministers and Big Dams', *Hindu*, 18 December 2005.

55 McCully, *Silenced Rivers* (1996; London, 2001), p. 3.

56 *Ibid.*, p. 3.

57 H. C. Moore, *Visit to the Works of the Proposed Birmingham Water Supply from the Elan Valley in Wales* (Hereford, 1896).

58 K. V. Rao and E. M. Gosschalk, 'The Case for Impounding Reservoirs: An Engineer's Viewpoint', *International Journal on Hydropower and Dams*, I/6 (1994).

59 Wallace Stegner, *The Sound of Mountain Water* (New York, 1969). Stegner was to write in 1980, 'Now I know enough not to speak admiringly of Reclamation dams without looking closely at their teeth', p. 61, 10.

60 Deborah Cadbury, *Seven Wonders of the Industrial World* (London, 2003), p. 293.

61 *Ibid.*, p. 326.

62 Chip Ward, Hope's Horizon: *Three Visions for Healing this American Land* (Washington, DC, 2004), p. 170.

63 Cadbury, *Seven Wonders of the Industrial World*, p. 330.

64 Donald C. Jackson, *Great American Bridges and Dams* (New York, 1988), p. 297.

65 Richard Guy Wilson, 'Machine-Age Iconography in the American West: The Design of Hoover Dam', *Pacific History Review*, LIV/4 (1985), reprinted in Donald C. Jackson, *Dams: Studies in the History of Civil Engineering* (Aldershot, 1997), p. 318.

66 *Ibid.*, p. 320.

67 Gordon B. Kaufmann, 'The Architecture of Boulder Dam', *Architectural Concrete*, III (1936) in Wilson, 'Machine-Age Iconography', p. 320.

68 Charles Inglis, *The Aesthetic Aspect of Civil Engineering Design* (London, 1945), p. 46.

69 Wilson, 'Machine-Age Iconography', p. 326.

70 *Ibid.*, p. 327.

71 Allen True, *Color and Decoration of the Boulder Dam*. Reclamation Era 1936 in Wilson, 'Machine-Age Iconography', p. 330.
72 Wilson, 'Machine-Age Iconography', p. 331.
73 Oskar Hansen, *The Sculptures at Hoover Dam* (Washington, DC, 1968).
74 Julian Rhinehart, 'The Grand Dam' in *Reclamation* (Boulder City, NV, 2004).
75 Wilson, 'Machine-Age Iconography', p. 334.
76 J. B. Priestley, 'Arizona Desert', *Harper's*, March 1937 in Wilson, 'Machine-Age Iconography', p. 335.
77 Joan Didion, *The White Album* (London, 1979), p. 198.
78 Richard Humphreys, *Futurism* (London, 1999), p. 48.
79 Bureau of Reclamation and Six Companies, *Boulder Dam: A Pictorial Record of Man's Conquest of the Colorado River* (film), 1935.
80 Didion, *White Album*, p. 201.
81 Donald Worster, *Hoover Dam: A Study in Domination under Western Skies: Nature and History in the American West* (New York, 1992) in Jackson, *Great American Bridges and Dams*, p. 351.
82 Nicholas J. Schnitter, *A History of Dams: The Useful Pyramids* (Rotterdam, 1994), p. 207.
83 Swiss National Committee on Large Dams, *Swiss Dams*, Edition for the 15th International Congress on Large Dams (Lausanne, 1985), p. 20.
84 *Ibid.*, p. 22.
85 R. Faure and J. de Castro San Román, 'The Arch: Enduring and Endearing', *Structural Concrete*, II/4 (December 2001), pp. 187–201.
86 www.snoarc.no (designed by the Norwegian architects Snøhetta).

4 Dam Failure

1 James Thurber, *The Thurber Carnival* (Middlesex, 1953), p. 162.
2 Nicholas J. Schnitter, *A History of Dams: The Useful Pyramids* (Rotterdam, 1994), p. 158.
3 Frederick Forsyth, *The Afghan* (London, 2006), p. 340.
4 Norman Smith, *A History of Dams* (London, 1971), p. 234.
5 Schnitter, *A History*, p. 2.
6 Geoffrey Binnie, *Early Victorian Water Engineers* (London, 1981), p. 50.
7 Holmfirth Express, *The Holmfirth Flood: The Bursting of the Bilberry Reservoir* (Holmfirth, 1910 [1991]), p. 22.
8 Binnie, *Early Victorian Water Engineers*, p. 63.
9 Geoffery Amey, *The Collapse of the Dale Dyke Dam 1864* (London, 1974), p. 52.
10 Binnie, *Early Victorian Water Engineers*, p. 269.
11 Smith, *A History*, p. 214.
12 *Ibid.*, p. 205.
13 Marie K. Nuschke, *The Dam that Could Not Break* (Coudersport, PA, 1960), p. 6.
14 Patrick Abercrombie, *The Preservation of Rural England* (Liverpool, 1926), pp. 51–2.
15 Charles F. Outland, *Man-made Disaster – The Story of St Francis Dam* (Ventura, CA, 2002), p. 237.
16 Margaret Leslie Davis, *Rivers in the Desert: William Mulholland and the Inventing of Los Angeles* (New York, 1993), p. 265. Davis quotes from John Walton (*Western Times and Water Wars* [Berkeley, 1992]) who saw the subplot of *Chinatown* as a

metaphor for the perceived rape of the Owens Valley.

17 *Ibid.*, p. 159.
18 *Ibid.*, p. 214.
19 Smith, *A History*, p. 239.
20 Louis J. Clements, *Teton Flood: June 5, 1976 Revisited* (Rexburg, ID, 1991), p. 8.
21 John Sweetman, *The Dambusters* (London, 2003), p. 30.
22 Edward Abbey, *The Monkey Wrench Gang* (New York, 1975).
23 Eric Halpin, 'Performance of the New Orleans Flood Protection System during Hurricane Katrina', *Hydropower & Dams*, XIII/4 (2006).
24 'Design Flaw Led to New Orleans Levee Break', *New Scientist*, 18 March 2006.

5 Dam Angry

1 William Wordsworth, *Guide to the Lakes* (1835; London, 1906), p. 11.
2 Harriet Ritvo, *Fighting for Thirlmere – The Roots of Environmentalism*, Essays on Science and Society, *Science* magazine (Washington and London, 2003).
3 Thirlmere Defence Association, *The Case Re-stated 1879*. The Association produced a number of pamphlets at this time; this one was produced as the Bill came before Parliament. For Wordsworth, the Lakes were 'a sort of national property in which every man has a right and interest', Mavis Batey et al., *Indignation: The Campaign for Conservation* (London, 2000), p. 18.
4 J. Gournett, *Thirlmere Defence Association 1877 Extracts from Leading Journals on the Manchester Water Scheme* (Windermere, 1878).
5 James Mitchell Clarke, *The Life and Adventures of John Muir* (San Diego, CA, 1979), p. 302.
6 John Muir, *The Yosemite* (New York, 1912), pp. 260–61.
7 *Ibid.*, p. 262.
8 www.sierraclub.
9 Frederick Law Olmsted, *Yosemite and the Mariposa Grove* (Report to the Library of Congress, 1865).
10 Marc Reisner, *Cadillac Dessert* (New York, 1990), p. 195.
11 *Ibid*, p. 198.
12 Amabel and Clough Williams-Ellis, *Headlong down the Years* (Liverpool, 1951), pp. 87–96.
13 Roy Gregory, 'The Cow Green Reservoir', in P. J. Smith, ed., *The Politics of Physical Resources* (Middlesex, 1975), p. 149.
14 Edward S. Flash, Jr, *The Battle of Cow Green: A Case Study on Water Resources in Britain*, Western Societies Program Occasional Paper No. 14 (Ithaca, NY, 1981), p. 30. Flash undertook research between January and July 1969 into the Cow Green scheme and in particular had access to BSBI (Botanical Society of the British Isles) information which has since become unavailable.
15 House of Commons, Minutes of Evidence to Select Committee, Tees Valley and Cleveland Water Bill, Evidence of Julius Kennard in examination by Peter Boydell QC for Promoters, 10 May 1966, Library of Centre for Ecology and Hydrology, Wallingford.
16 *Ibid.*
17 'Floods for Industry', *Northern Echo* (Darlington), 11 December 1964.
18 'Upper Teesdale's New Reservoir', *Northern Echo* (Darlington), 9 January 1965.

19 'Botanists Prepare to Fight Teesdale Reservoir', *Northern Echo* (Darlington), 30 July 1965.

20 'Upper Teesdale's New Reservoir', *Northern Echo* (Darlington), 9 January 1965.

21 Richard Crossman, *The Diaries of a Cabinet Minister*, vol. I: *Minister of Housing, 1964–66* (London, 1975), p. 503.

22 Durham County Council, Minutes of Meeting between Tees Valley and Cleveland Water Board, Sandeman, Kennard and Partners, Westmorland County Council, North Riding of Yorkshire County Council, Durham County Council and Barnard Castle Rural District Council, 23 December 1965, Cow Green File 3, Durham County Council Planning Department, County Hall, Durham, 1965.

23 Crossman, *The Diaries*, p. 503.

24 House of Commons, Minutes of Evidence to Select Committee, Tees Valley and Cleveland Water Bill, Evidence of Frederick Gibberd in examination by Frank Layfield for Promoters and Harold Marnham QC for the Petitioners, 18 May 1966, Library of Centre for Ecology and Hydrology, Wallingford.

25 Flash, *The Battle*, p. 72.

26 House of Lords, Minutes of Evidence to Select Committee, Tees Valley and Cleveland Water Bill, Evidence of Frederick Gibberd in examination by Frank Layfield for Promoters, *Hansard*, 7 December 1966.

27 David Bellamy, personal communication with the author, 2000.

28 Arundhati Roy, 'Dam Buster', *Guardian*, 28 July 2001.

29 SSNN Ltd, *Sardar Sarovar Project on River Narmada* (Gujarat, 1999).

30 WCD, *South Asia Consultation* (Colombo, Sri Lanka, 1998).

31 Chip Ward, *Hope's Horizon: Three Visions for Healing this American Land* (Washington, DC, 2004), p. 151.

32 *Ibid.*, p. 189.

33 www.americanrivers.org

34 Marc Reisner, *The Age of Dams and Its Legacy* (Columbia University, 2000); www.earthinstitute.columbia.edu

35 WWF, *Dam Right: WWF's Dams Initiative – To Dam or Not to Dam?* (Godalming, 2005).

36 John Briscoe, 'Financing NT2 in Laos: A World Bank Perspective', *HRW* (March 2006).

6 What Environment?

1 Brian Rofe, *Reservoirs – An Environmental Gain* (London, 1995).

2 World Commission on Dams, *Dams and Development* (London, 2000).

3 Trevor Turpin, *Environmental Impacts of Dams: The Changing Approach to Mitigation* in *Dams 2000*, Proceedings of the Biennial Conference of the British Dams Society (Wallingford, 2000), p. 227.

4 'Opposition to Water Bill', *Birmingham Daily Post*, 8 March 1892.

5 James Mansergh, Proof of Evidence in Support of the Bill. Birmingham Corporation Water, 1892.

6 L. H. Evans and R. Darlington, *Rhiyades and the Highlands and Lakes of Mid-Wales* (Rhayader, 1907), pp. 7–15.

7 *Ibid.*, p. 8.

8 Sylvia Crowe, *Tomorrow's Landscape* (London, 1956), p. 70.

9 *Ibid*, p. 69.
10 Barbara A. Carroll, 'Sustainable Development: An Eclectic Review', in *Chartered Institution of Water and Environmental Management. International Directory* (Tyne and Wear, 2003).
11 Crowe, *Tomorrow's Landscapes*, p. 158.
12 Tom Turner, *Landscape Planning and Environmental Impact Design*, second edn (London, 1998), p. 175.
13 J. A. Picken, 'The Chew Stoke Reservoir Scheme' *Journal of the Institution of Water Engineers*, XI/4 (July 1957), pp. 333–82.
14 *Ibid*.
15 Tom Turner, *Landscape Planning* (London, 1987), p. 36.
16 'The Somerset Lake District: Its Beauty Will Never Be Spoiled', *Western Daily Press*, 8 September 1955.
17 Lesley Ross, ed., *Before the Lake: Memories of the Chew Valley* (Harptree, 2004), p. 167.
18 A.J.H. Winder, R. G. Cole and G. E. Bowyer, 'The Empingham Reservoir Project (Rutland Water)', *Procs ICE*, LXXVIII (1985), p. 78.
19 D. Coats and N. Ruffle, 'The Kielder Water Scheme' *Procs. ICE*, LXXVIII (1982); discussion LXXVIII (1983), pp. 127–48.
20 David Howarth, *The Shadow of the Dam* (London, 1961), p. 7.
21 Frank Clements, *Kariba: The Struggle with the River God* (London, 1959), p. 184.
22 Eric Robins and Ronald Legge, *Animal Dunkirk – The Story of Lake Kariba and 'Operation Noah', the Greatest Animal Rescue since the Ark* (London, 1959), p. 100.
23 Tom Little, *High Dam at Aswan* (London, 1965), p. 16.
24 *Ibid*., pp. 156–36.
25 Jack Lewin and Yuil Eprim, *Venice Flood Barriers* (London, 2004).
26 Frederick Gibberd, 'The Landscape of Reservoirs', *Journal of Institution of Water Engineers*, XV (1961), pp. 83–115.
27 Sir Crispin Tickell, *Resurgence Anniversary Meeting* (Oxford, 2006).
28 'Dam puts Shanghai wetlands at sea's mercy', *New Scientist*, 19 April 2006, p. 22.
29 Fred Pearce, *When the Rivers Run Dry* (London, 2006), p. 178.
30 Robert Freer, 'The Three Gorges Project on the Yangtze River in China', *Civil Engineering*, CXLIV (February 2001).
31 Lin Chuxue, 'Three Gorges Project for Sustainable Development of the Yangtze Valley', *Hydropower & Dams*, XIII/1 (2006).
32 Chip Ward, *Hope's Horizon*, p. 190.
33 ICOLD Code of Ethics, adopted 17 June 2006 in Barcelona.

Postscript

1 Fred Pearce, *When the Rivers Run Dry* (London, 2006), p. 159.
2 F. Lempiérière, R. Lafitte, in Berga et al., ed, 'The Role of Dams in the XXI Century to Achieve a Sustainable Development Target', in *Dams and Reservoirs, Societies and Environment in the 21st Century* (London, 2006), p. 1070.

Select Bibliography

Binnie, Geoffrey, *Early Victorian Water Engineers* (London, 1981)
Cadbury, Deborah, *Seven Wonders of the Industrial World* (London, 2003)
Cosgrove, Denis, and Geoff Petts, *Water, Engineering and Landscape* (London, 1990)
Goldsmith, Edward and Nicholas Hildyard, *The Social and Environmental Effects of Large Dams* (Wadebridge, 1984)
Grossman, Elizabeth, *Watershed: The Undamming of America* (New York, 2002)
Jackson, Donald C., *Dams: Studies in the History of Civil Engineering* (Aldershot, 1997)
—, *Great American Bridges and Dams* (New York, 1988)
Lowry, William R., *Dam Politics: Restoring America's Rivers* (Georgetown, 2003)
McCully, Patrick, *Silenced Rivers* (1996; London, 2001)
Murkoff, Bruce, *Waterborne* (New York, 2004)
Pearce, Fred, *The Dammed* (London, 1992)
—, *When the Rivers Run Dry* (London, 2006)
Reisner, Marc, *Cadillac Desert: The American West and Its Disappearing Water* (London, 1990)
Roy, Arundhati, *The Cost of Living* (Toronto, 1999)
Schnitter, Nicholas J., *A History of Dams: The Useful Pyramids* (Rotterdam, 1994)
Smith, Norman, *A History of Dams* (London, 1971)
Sullivan, Dick, *Navvyman* (Ely, 1983)
Turner, Tom, *Landscape Planning and Environmental Impact Design* (London, 1998)
Ward, Chip, *Hope's Horizon: Three Visions for Healing this American Land* (Washington, DC, 2004)
World Commission on Dams, *Dams and Development: A New Framework for Decision-Making* (London, 2000)
Worster, Donald, *Rivers of Empire: Water, Aridity and the Growth of the American West* (New York, 1985)

Acknowledgements

Librarians and archivists are the unsung heroes of the researcher, but I must make particular mention of the staff at the library and archives of the Institution of Civil Engineers in London. Special thanks too for their support, advice, tolerance (in varying degrees) and inspiration to: S. R. Aruppola; G. Bandaranayake; David Bellamy; Chris Binnie; John Brady; Angus Buchanan; Phil Burgi; Stuart Burroughs; Anna Chalmers; Mollie Clough; Bill Craig; Tom Douglas; Hank Falvey; Ravi Fernando; Barbara Frears; Warren Frizell; Jackie Hayes; Jonathan Hinks; Colin Hunt; Geoff Ingham; David Johnson; Michael Kennard; Bala Krishnan; Jack Lewin; D.L.O. Mendis; Dave Pearce; Nicholas Pearson; Christopher Pound; Bernard Priest; Cliff Pugh; Parthsarathy Ramanujam; Martin Ross; Alexander Semenov; Amanda Starr; Tom Turner and Neil Whiter.

While much material for this book has been gained from visits to dams and reservoirs throughout Europe, Asia, India and Sri Lanka, the Middle East and the US and from conversations and communications with engineers in these areas, most of the credit for its inspiration must go to writers who have gone before me. Their works are cited in the references and select bibliography. Readers are particularly directed to the classic works on the history of dams by Geoffrey Binnie, Nicholas Schnitter, Norman Smith and Donald Jackson; on dams and the environment by Patrick McCully and Fred Pearce; and on the American West by Marc Reisner. While not attempting to take sides or issue with their respective views, I have tried through the various themes suggested by the Objekt series to draw together the wide range of issues raised by dams.

I am particularly grateful to Alan Ervine, Professor of Engineering at Glasgow University, and to Jim Millmore, past Chairman of the British Dam Society, for checking the draft for factual errors and for their helpful suggestions.

On a personal note, I wish to acknowledge the guidance and support of Professors Christopher Wood and Michael Hebbert at the University of Manchester, and, of course, of Barbara Carroll, Visiting Professor of Sustainable Development at Glasgow University and my muse, who asked for stories about dams but probably didn't expect the leeches.

Photographic Acknowledgements

The author and publishers wish to express their thanks to the below sources of illustrative material and/or permission to reproduce it:

From *Afsluitdijk* (Lelystad, Netherlands, c. 1982): p. 49 (left); courtesy of the artist (Steve Bell): p. 194; photos author: pp. 6, 8, 9, 11, 14, 17, 28, 32, 40, 41, 104, 107, 109, 110, 111, 114, 136, 182 (foot), 213, 222, 226; collection of the author: pp. 81, 89, 94, 98, 102, 112, 118, 166, 167; from *Building News* (7 May, 1858): p. 67; courtesy Cardiff Bay Development Corporation: p. 187; photo Barbara Carroll: p. 36; Anna Chalmers: p. 237; from *Dam the Thames* (Effingham, Surrey, 1935): p. 49 (top right); photo courtesy of Hydro-Québec: p. 113; from the *Illustrated London News*: pp. 19 (23 February 1889), 147 (26 March 1864); photo Frances Benjamin Johnston/Library of Congress, Washington, DC (Prints and Photographs Division, Frances Benjamin Johnston Collection, LC-USZ6-1674): p. 57; photo Jack Lewin: p. 224; photo courtesy Mahaweli Authority, Sri Lanka: p. 195; from *Popular Mechanics Magazine* (March, 1946): p. 49 bottom right; photo Christopher Pound: p. 42; photo Bernard Priest: p. 35; photo Gunter R. Reitz: p. 223; photo courtesy River Dove Water Board: p. 225 (right); photo courtesy Sardar Sarovar Narmada Nigam Ltd: p. 188; from D. Saslavsky, *Dnieprostroi: The Biggest Dam in the World* (Moscow, 1932): p. 125; from *Scientific American*: pp. 38 (20 January 1900), 85 (4 May 1901); photos Sipa Press/Rex Features: pp. 13 (587744C), 231 (419136C); photo courtesy of Snoart: p. 139; photo courtesy of South West Water: p. 120; from R. Eustace Tickell, *The Vale of Nantgwillt* (London, 1894): p. 77; photo US National Archives, Still Picture Branch: p. 135 (National Park Service 79-AAB-1); photo Barbara Wallhouse: p. 225 (left); photo courtesy of the Water Supply and Sewerage Corporation of Athens: p. 97.

Index

Abbeystead Dam (Lancs) 96
Abercrombie, Patrick 116, 155
Afsluitdijk (Neths) 47, *48*
Akosombo Dam (Ghana) 24, *25*
Alcantrilla Dam (Spain) 142
Allt-na-Lairige Dam (Argyll) 43
Alresford Dam (Hants) *32*
Amir Dam (Iran) 19
Anyox Dam (Canada) 93
Appleton Dam (USA) 40
Ardingly Reservoir (Sussex) 119, 226
Assiut Dam (Egypt) 23, 30
Aswan Dams (Egypt) 13, *14*, 23, 24, 163,
    218
    design and construction 30, *31*, 84,
    85, 86–8, 126
    environmental impact 216–21,
    222–3
Ataturk Dam (Turkey) 67
Austin Dam, Pennsylvania (USA) 152,
    153
Austin Dam, Texas (USA) 40, 152
Aymard, Maurice 151

Babtie, Shaw and Morton 162, 213
Baker, Sir Benjamin 69–70, 84, 86–7
Bakethin Dam (Northumb) 213, *214*
Balderhead Reservoir (Dur) 181, 184
Balojaque Dam (Mexico) 93
Banqiao Dam (China) 161–2
Bateman, J. F. La Trobe 58, 61, 69,
    145–7, 149, 170–1
Bazalgette, Joseph 49, 68

Bear Valley Dam (USA) 27–8, *91*, 92
Bellamy, David 183, 185, 191
Betwa Dam (India) 84
Bewl Water (Kent) 119, 226
Bhakra Dam (India) 23, *24*, 127–8
Big Creek Dam (USA) 90, 91
Big Meadows Dam (USA) 92
Bilberry Dam (Yorks) 143–4, *145*, 146–7
Binnie, Sir Alexander 36, 61, 80, 116
Binnie, Christopher 116
Binnie, Geoffrey 58, 143
Binnie, William 95
Blackbrook Dam (Leics) 142
Blagdon Lake (Som) 211
Blenheim (Oxon) 22, 59
Bough Beech Reservoir (Kent) 119, 226
Boulder City (USA) 10, 99, 100
Boulé, Auguste 84
Bouzey Dam (France) 79, 86, 151–2
Boyds Corner Dam (USA) 111
Bratsk Dam (Russia) 125–6
Brindley, James 32–3
Broad Oak Reservoir (Kent) 226
Brown, Frank E. 27, 28–9, 91
Brown, Lancelot 'Capability' 22–3, 59,
    107
Buchanan, Angus 58, 60, 61
Buchanan, Dorothy 95
By, Lieut-Col. John 33

Caban Coch (Powys) *6*, *17*, 78, 80, 83
Cardiff Bay (Glam) 186, *187*
Carsington Dam (Derbys) 162

Cave Creek Dam (USA) 93, *94*
Chabot, Anthony 65
Chalillo Dam (Belize) 192
Cheddar Reservoir (Som) 210
Chew Valley Lake (Som) 208–12
Chiloquin Dam (USA) 198
Churchill, Winston 13–14, 22, 84, 102,
    233
Claerwen Dam (Powys) 17, 75–6, 83, 110,
    115, 207
Coedty Dam (Gwynedd) *154*, 155
Collin, Alexandre 64
Colvin, Brenda 121
Conybeare, Henry 67–8, 149
Coolidge Dam (USA) 35, *112*
Coquett Ironworks (Northumb) 59–60
Cotton, Arthur 68
Coulomb, Charles A. 64, 69
Cow Green Dam (UK) 118, 181, *182*,
    183–6, 204
Cowlyd Dam (Gwynedd) 155
Coyne, André 112, 159
Cray Dam (Powys) 82
Croton Dams (USA) 37, *38*, 39, 113–14
Crowe, Sylvia 115, 119, 121, 207, 208,
    226
Crystal Springs Dam (USA) 96, 106, *111*
Cubitt, Thomas (Cubitts) 61, 62
Cubitt, Sir William 62
Cwm Elan (Powys) 16, 76, *77*

Dale Dyke Dam (Yorks) 68, *147*, 148–9
Danah Dam (Yemen) 141–2
Daniel Johnson Dam (Canada) 112, *113*
Deacon, George 17–18, 58, 87, 170
Delocre, Emile 65, 152
Delta Plan 49
Derwent Dam (Derbys) *166*
Derwent Dam (Dur) *110*, 225
Diemel Dam (Germany) 165, 167
Diggle Dam (Lancs) 143
Digley Reservoir (Yorks) 147
Dneprovsk Dam (Ukraine) 123, 124
Dnieprostroi (Russia) 123–4, *125*, 163–4
Dooley, Dan 96

Eastwood, John S. 28, 89–94, 111
Echo Park Dam (USA) 196–7

Eder Dam (Germany) 165, 166, 167, 168
Eigiau Dam (Gwynedd) 154
Elan Valley (Powys) *6*, 7, 8, 11, 16, *17*
    design and construction 58, 59,
    73–9, *80–1*, 82–3, 110
    environmental impact *77*, 115,
    206–7, 227
Ennepe Dam (Germany) 165, 167, 168
Evans, Oliver 33

Faber, Oscar 115
Fish Creek Dam (USA) 92
Flaming Gorge Dam (USA) 197
Foel Valve Tower (Powys) 16, *17*, 79–80,
    81
Forest de Bélidor, Bernard 63, 64
Fort Peck Dam (USA) 26, *27*, *65*, 66,
    107
Fowler, Charles 112–14, 118
Franklin Dam (Tasmania) 190–2
Frears, Barbara 225
Freeman, John R. 92
Furens Dam (France) 46, 65

Garrison Dam (USA) 177–8, *179*
Gatun Dam (Panama) 21, 34
Gautier, Henri 63–4
Gebel Anlia Dam (Sudan) 23
Gibberd, Frederick 117, 118, 184, 185,
    225
Gicot, H. 137
Glen Canyon Dam (USA) 104, 168,
    196–7, *198*
Glencorse Dam (Edinburgh) 34, *35*
Glendoe Dam (Highland) 44
Gordon, Lewis 69
Gore, William 87
Gosschalk, Ed 122–3, 126
Graeff, Auguste 65
Grafham Water scheme (Cambs) 117
Grand Coulee Dam (USA) 50, 53, *98*,
    99–101, *102–3*
Grande Dixence (Switz) 137
Grosbois Dam (France) 64
Grundy, John 59, 60

Habra Dam (Algeria) 151
Hansen, Oskar 10, 11, 131, 134

Hatton, T. Chalkley 152
Haweswater Dam (Cumbria) *104*, 109, 172, 230
Hawksley, Thomas 58, 61, 62, 63, 66, 149
Hawksley, Watson 212
Henne Dam (Germany) 165, 166-7
Hetch Hetchy (USA) 7, 172, 173-5
Hill, George Henry 172
Hill, H. Prescot 95
Holden, Charles 115-16
Hollywood Dam (USA) 158, *159*
Hongrin Dam (Switz) 137, 138
Hoover Dam (USA) 10, *11*, 21-2, 26, 53, 234
    construction 97-9, 100, 105
    design 107, 111, 128, 129-32, *133*, 134, *135-6*, 137
    environmental impact 163
Huai River Dam (China) 163
Hume Lake Dam (USA) 91
hydropower 39-46

Ilisu Dam (Turkey) 193-5
Inguri Dam (Georgia) 125
Institution of Civil Engineers 36, 61, 84, 95, 114-15, 117
Iron Gate Dam (USA) 198
irrigation 26-30
Itaipu Dam (Brazil/Paraguay) 44, *45*, *46*, 195

Jackson, Matthew 149
Java (Jordan) 10, 57
Jellicoe, Sir Geoffrey 108, 118
Jessop, William 32, 59, 61, 62, 142
Johnston, Tom 101-2
Jones Falls Dam (Canada) 33

Kariba Dam (Zambia/Zimb) 163, 214, *215*, 216
Kaufmann, Gordon B. 10, 130-6
Kennard, Julius 103, 183
Kesis Gölü Dam (Turkey) 152
Khadjoo Dam (Iran) 19, 20, *21*
Kielder Water (Northumb) 118-19, 213-14, 225
Kingairloch Dam (Highland) 44

Kinlochleven scheme (Highland) 42
Koyna Dam (India) 163

Laudot Dam (France) 30-1
Lawson, John 74
Leather, George 61, 144, 145, 146, 147
Leather, John Towlerton 61, 147
Leather, John Wignall 61
Lely, Cornelis 47
Leslie, James 61, 149
Levy, Maurice 152
Lister Dam (Germany) 165, 167
Loch Katrine (Stirling) 69
Loch Sloy Dam (Argyll) *43*, 102
Lovejoy, Derek 119

McCullough, Fred W. 95
MacDonald, Sir Murdoch 86, 87-8
Maentwrog scheme (Gwynedd) 43
Malpasset Dam (France) 159
Mangla Dam (Pakistan) 23
Mansergh, James 7, 58, 61, 74, 235
    Elan Valley scheme 16, 74-6, 78, 79-80, 206-7, 227
Mantinea Dam (Greece) 163
Marathon Dam (Greece) *97*
Marchlyn Dam (Gwynedd) 116
Martínez de Lara, Géronimo 143
Mattmark Dam (Switz) 168-9
Mauvoisin Dam (Switz) 137
Medlow Dam (Aust) 36-7, *37*
Megget Reservoir (Borders) 120, *226*
Mekong River Basin 200
Memphis Dam (Egypt) 141
Merwin Dam (USA) 96
Mir Alam Dam (India) 35, *36*
Möhne Dam (Germany) 165, 166, *167*, 168
Mont Saint-Michel (France) 199
Montague, Adrian 117
Moody, R. C. 145-6
Morman Flat Dam (USA) *66*
Morris, William E. 149
Morris Dam (USA) 97
Mountain Dell Dam (USA) 92
Mud Mountain Dam (USA) 46
Mulholland, William 156, 157-8
Mulholland Dam (USA) 158, *159*

Nagarjunasagar Dam (India) 103
Nam Theun 2 Dam (Laos) 201–2
Nantgwillt (Powys) 16, 76, 77, 78, 81
navigation 30–4
Nealon, Kenneth 210
New Orleans (USA) 13, 169
Nobel, Alfred 66
Norris Dam (USA) *50*
Nurek Dam (Tajikistan) 105, 125

Oder Dam (Germany) 66
Ogochi Dam (Japan) 126, *127*
Olmsted, Frederick Law 176
Ordunte Dam (Spain) 163
O'Shaughnessy Dam (USA) 113, *114*,
    175–6
Otay Creek Dam (USA) 29

Pak Mun Dam (Thailand) 201
Parakrama Samudra Dam (Sri Lanka) 21
Parker Dam (USA) 99
Pearson, Nicholas 226
Pen-y-Gareg (Powys) *8*, 76, *80*, 207
Pennycuick, John 68, 70, 72, 73
Pergau Dam (Malaysia) 193, 194
Periyar Dam (India) 27, *28*, 68, 70–3
Pérolles Dam (Switz) 111
Pitlochry Dam (Perth) *230*
Plitvice Lakes (Croatia) *56*, 57
Presa de Rules Dam (Spain) 96–7
Puentes Dam (Spain) 142–3
Pune Dam (India) 67

Queen Mother Reservoir (London) 119–20

Rankine, W.J.M. 27, 58, 68–70, 152
Rawlinson, Sir Robert 61, 73, 74–5,
    148–9, 235
Reisner, Marc 104, 129, 199–200
Rennie, John 32, 34, 58, 59, 61, 131, 149
Ringedals Dam (Norway) *40–1*, 42
Riquet, Pierre-Paul 30–1
Rofe, Henry and John 73
Rofe, Kennard and Lapworth 33, 73, 226
Rogun Dam (Tajikistan) 105, 125, 126
Rolt, L.T.C. 58
Roosevelt Dam (USA) *54*, *55*, 113
Royal Engineers 33, 60, 68, 145

Rudyard Embankment Dam (Staffs) 32, 34
Rutland Water (Rut) 119, 212, *213*, 226
Ryves, Major 68

St Francis Dam (USA) 140, 156–8
St Petersburg barrier (Russia) 125
Saint-Ferreol Dam (France) 30
Sakuma Dam (Japan) *126*
San Gabriel Dam (USA) 46
San Mateo Dam (USA) 140–1
Sandeman, Edward 95
Sandeman, Kennard and Partners 181
Sant' Elia, Antonio 131, 132, 136
Sardar Sarovar Dam (India) 12, 187, *188*,
    189–90
Savage, John L. 97, 130
Sazilly, J. Augustin Torterne de 64–5,
    152
Schnitter, Nicholas 36, 61, 137, 138, 141
Schussler, Hermann 90, 96, 106, 111
Schuyler, James D. 29, 91, 92
Scott-Moncrieff, Colin 83, 84, 217
Semenza, Carlo 160
Sennar Dam (Sudan) 23
Sepid Rood Dam (Iran) *20*
Severn Barrage 43, *44*
Shasta Dam (USA) 99
Shimantan Dam (China) 161–2
Silent Valley Dam (N Ireland) 94, *95*, 96
Simpson, James 58, 149
Skelmorlie Reservoir Dam (N Ayrs) 155
Smeaton, John 34, 58, 59–61, 62
Smith, Norman 29–30, 39, 64, 83, 141,
    149, 151, 159
Society of Civil Engineers 60–1
Son La Dam (Vietnam) 201
Sorpe Dam (Germany) 165, 166, 167,
    168
South Fork Dam (USA) 149, *150*
Staunton Harold Valve Tower (Leics) *225*
Staveley, Charles 142
Stourhead (Wilts) 106
Studley Royal (Yorks) 108
Sweetwater Dam (USA) 28, *29*
Syncrude Tailings Dam (Canada) 52

Tamar Dam (Devon) 33
Tarbela Dam (Pakistan) 105

Telford, Thomas 32,
Tennessee Valley Autho.
   52-3, 101, 126
Terzaghi, Karl von 88
Teton River Dam (USA) 160-1
Thames Barrier 8, *9*, 48, 49-50
Thames reservoirs 9-10, 207-8
Thirlmere Dam (Cumbria) 107, *171*, 172
Thornley, D. G. 118
Three Gorges Dam (China) 12, *13*, 24,
   105
   design and construction *48*, 50-2, 97
   environmental impact 200, 202, 227,
   228-9, *231*
Tickell, Eustace 76-7
Tolla Dam (Corsica) 159
Torricelli, Giacomo 84
Trawsfynnd Dam (Gwynedd) 43
Trento (Italy), tailings dam 161, 162
Tryweryn scheme (Gwynedd) 117, 118,
   225
Tunnel End Dam (Lancs) 143
Tunstall Dam (Dur) 66-7
Turner, Tom 110, 121, 208

Upper Otay Dam (USA) 29

Vaiont Dam (Italy) 12-13, 137, 160
Vehar Dam (India) *67*
Venice (Italy) 222-3, *224*
Victoria Dam (Sri Lanka) *195*, 196
Villarreal de Berriz, Don Pedro Bernardo
   64
Vire Dam (France) *107*
Volkhovstroi Dam (Russia) 123, 124
Vyrnwy (Powys) 17-18, *19*, 58, 170, 171

Wade, L.A.B. 36
Wallis, Barnes Neville 164-5, 166, 168
Wank, Roland A. 53, 126
Webber Creek Dam (USA) 93
Weieringermeer (Neths) 47
Willcocks, Sir William 30, 83-6, 87-8,
   218
Williamson, James 102
Wimbleball Dam (Som) *120*
Woodhead Dam (Derbys) 143
World Commission on Dams 12, 190,